W9-CCW-358

Creative Conflict Resolution

More Than 200 Activities for Keeping
Peace in the Classroom

 **Good Year Books**

are available for preschool through grade 12 and for
every basic curriculum subject plus many enrichment
areas. For more Good Year Books, contact your local
bookseller or educational dealer. For a complete
catalog with information about other Good Year Books,
please write:

Good Year Books
Department GYB
1900 East Lake Avenue
Glenview, Illinois 60025

Creative Conflict Resolution

More Than 200 Activities for Keeping Peace in the Classroom

William J. Kreidler

Scott, Foresman and Company

Glenview, Illinois London

To my mother and father,
and my good friends at
the Beacon Hill Friends Meeting

ISBN: 0-673-15642-7

Copyright © 1984 William J. Kreidler.
All Rights Reserved.
Printed in the United States of America.

16 17 18-MAL-94 93 92

No part of this book may be reproduced in any form or by any means,
except those portions intended for classroom use, without permission in
writing from the publisher.

LB
1537
.K74
1984

Preface

Every classroom has conflict. If you would like to use the conflict in your classroom productively, then welcome to *Creative Conflict Resolution*. This book reflects my belief that conflicts can be reduced through the establishment of a caring classroom community, and that the conflict remaining can be used for learning.

Creative Conflict Resolution is an approach to classroom management. It is not a curriculum etched in stone. In many ways, this book is like a kit containing some plans and many tools. It is my hope that these tools will enable you to build something I call the peaceable classroom, but how your peaceable classroom finally looks is up to you.

Each chapter in this book begins with information to help you better understand the approach. The second part of each chapter contains descriptions of activities for implementing the approach. The activities are grouped according to the topics discussed in the chapters. You can choose those you think will best meet the needs of your students. For each activity, grade levels are suggested, but many are adaptable higher or lower. When grade levels are listed in parentheses, suggestions for adapting the activity are included. You know best what your students need. Each activity description also includes a list of materials and discussion starters, if appropriate. The symbol 🍎 indicates suggested variations, extensions, or comments on the activity.

Also included throughout the book are exercises you can use to examine your classroom, your students' behavior, and yourself in light of the material being discussed. The purpose of these exercises is to make the material more relevant and useful to you and your classroom. They were developed for, and refined by, use in my Peaceable Classroom Workshops, and many teachers tell me they have found them useful. I am aware, however, that some people dislike such exercises. I have designed them so that you may simply skim them if you choose. They will still work if they are skimmed, but I encourage you to take time to think about them.

The model of the peaceable classroom in this book is based on the pioneering peace education work of two groups, the Nonviolence and Children Program in Philadelphia, and the Children's Creative Response to Conflict Project in New York. Their respective books, *A Manual on Nonviolence and Children* and *The Friendly Classroom for a Small Planet* (see Bibliography of Resources), reflect many years of experience training people of all ages in the theory and technique of nonviolent conflict resolution. I am indebted to these groups not only for a theoretical framework but also for getting me started in creative conflict resolution with children.

I began, rather tentatively, in my own classroom, playing cooperative games and doing cooperation activities. Somewhat surprised by the success of these, I began to work on improving communication in my classroom and trying various conflict resolution techniques. Before long, there were clear and measurable improvements in the way the children related, worked together, and responded to conflict.

Having seen success in my own classroom, I talked with other teachers and began giving teacher training workshops. At the same time, I began graduate work in curriculum development, specifically to explore further this area of peace education.

As I surveyed the available literature on resolving classroom conflict, as I conducted workshops and worked with other teachers, and as I continued my own teaching, it became clear to me that there was a need for a closer look at classroom conflict, a guide to more thorough training in its resolution, and a clearer approach to building classroom community. With this book I attempt to fill that need, building on previous work in this field.

Acknowledgments

As I worked on this book, many people helped and encouraged me. I would like to thank some of them here. For their ideas and constructive criticism, I thank Kathy Allen, Birgit Arons, Bill Beneville, Frances Crowe, Sue Devokaitis, Sandy Eccleston, Bill Graf, John Grassi, Jane Guise, Gerry Moore, Sukie Rice, Fran Schmidt, Beverly Woodward, Gail Wooten, and Liz Yeats. I thank the Walpole Public School System, particularly superintendent Robert Bassett and principals Bill Graf, Harold Varney, and Hal LeBlanc, for their patience and support. Special thanks to Sheila Edlestein, Katherine McGolderick, and Marilyn Richter.

Contents

Introduction

Making Peace

A teacher is a peacemaker. It's part of the job. Perhaps you and I never thought of ourselves as quite that; perhaps we're not even sure what peacemaking means. But conflicts occur in our classrooms, and we are expected to respond to them and restore peace, or at least order. That makes us peacemakers.

Of course, how good we are at making peace is something else again. Rarely is there anything in our education to help us understand conflict, or training in the skills necessary for making peace.

Here is one teacher's story. See if it sounds at all familiar.

Tim Hall is a caring and competent teacher, but this morning as he moves about, readying his kindergarten classroom for the children's arrival, he is admonishing himself for his behavior lately. He has been, he feels, too impatient, yelling far too much and being generally insensitive to the children. "Today," he vows silently, "I'm not going to yell once."

In a few minutes the children enter, greeting Tim with big smiles. Jeanne hands Tim a note—Jeanne frequently has long notes for Tim, filled with her mother's concern for Jeanne's progress. Tim sets the note on his desk, wondering how he will respond to it.

For show and tell, one of the boys has brought a Superman doll. "Boys shouldn't play with dolls," Stephanie declares, and several of the children nod vigorously. Tim begins a discussion to counter this statement, but the children are restless and clearly unconvinced. Tim senses that it is time to move on. "Well, in this room, boys and girls can play with whatever they want," he states flatly, and changes the subject.

Before long, Tim has all the children productively engaged and is settling a group on the rug to work on number concepts. John doesn't want to sit next to Colleen. Tim considers discussing this but decides to let it go. John changes his seat.

Meanwhile, the noise level in the rest of the room is rising. Three children are playing a reading readiness game, and Brian is gloating because he is farther along. Angela is sullenly playing with clay. She reaches for more, but it's all gone. "Hey, you guys took all the clay! Mr. Hall, they took all the clay." Tim leaves his group, distributes the clay equitably, and throws in a few words about sharing.

"Boys and girls, it's getting very noisy in here," he adds for the benefit of the rest of the class.

"Mr. Hall, they won't let me play at the sandbox," complains James. On his way to the sandbox, Tim notices that his group on the rug has blithely forgotten all about working. "Let him play," Tim snaps at the sandbox group. Then, raising his voice slightly, he tries to quiet the class once again. Two boys continue to make noise in a corner.

"Boys! If I have to speak to you again, you'll have to stay in for recess," Tim says. Tim returns to his small group. Half of them can't seem to grasp the concept, and half of them grasped it immediately and now in their boredom have begun squirming and tickling each other.

The room has gotten noisy once again, and Tim can barely hear Carolyn as she gives, as usual, a wrong answer. As he stands, ready to bellow his class into submission, Tim sees James pick up a handful of sand and fling it into the face of Susan, whose father is school board president. School has been in session one hour, and Tim is grimly aware that he is about to break his vow of that morning.

Tim's classroom is only slightly exaggerated. I know, because during my first year of teaching, all those incidents happened in my room. The types of conflict that occurred in Tim's room occur in all classrooms, from kindergarten on up.

The fact is that teachers encounter an astounding number and variety of conflicts every day. Overt conflicts and subtle ones. Conflicts over big issues and small. Sometimes they end with laughter, sometimes with hurt feelings or black eyes.

The purpose of this book is to help teachers and others who work with children do three things:

1. increase their understanding of conflict and its resolution and expand their repertoire of peacemaking skills

2. examine their behavior and attitudes to assess how they contribute to classroom conflict and its resolution

3. work on establishing a sense of classroom community that will not only reduce conflict but also help children respond creatively, constructively, and nonviolently to conflict—in short, to build the peaceable classroom

What is the peaceable classroom? The term probably suggests something different to each reader. In this book, the concept is not related to noise levels, class size, or open vs. traditional teaching styles. It refers to a classroom that is also a warm and caring community, where there are five qualities present:

1. *Cooperation.* Children learn to work together and trust, help, and share with each other.

2. *Communication.* Children learn to observe carefully, communicate accurately, and listen sensitively.

3. *Tolerance.* Children learn to respect and appreciate people's differences and to understand prejudice and how it works.

4. *Positive emotional expression.* Children learn to express feelings, particularly anger and frustration, in ways that are not aggressive or destructive, and children learn self-control.

5. *Conflict resolution.* Children learn the skills of responding creatively to conflict in the context of a supportive, caring community.

The dividing lines between these components are often difficult to draw in practice; I have drawn them here for convenience of discussion. The strength of the model comes from its interrelatedness—its synergistic nature. That is to say, the whole is greater than the sum of its parts. Similarly, there is no particular sequence to establishing these qualities in the classroom community, although laying the groundwork of cooperation, communication, tolerance, and positive emotional expression will do much to reduce classroom conflicts and resolve them when they do arise.

Creative conflict resolution does not try to eliminate classroom conflict. That is neither possible nor desirable. Instead, it aims to reduce conflict and to help you and your students deal more effectively and constructively with the conflicts that do occur.

Causes of Classroom Conflict

What causes conflicts that spring up in your classroom? If you look closely, you can see that many of these conflicts are symptomatic of deeper problems. These problems are the true causes of classroom conflict; and, by analyzing them, you can begin to use conflict productively. These causes can be grouped loosely into six categories, based on the peaceable classroom model just presented.

1. *Competitive atmosphere.* When there is a highly competitive atmosphere in a classroom, students learn to work against rather than with each other. Conflicts frequently arise out of:

> an attitude of everyone for himself or herself
>
> lack of skill in working in groups
>
> students feeling compelled to win in interactions because losing results in loss of self-esteem
>
> lack of trust in the teacher or classmates
>
> competition at inappropriate times

2. *Intolerant atmosphere.* An intolerant classroom is an unfriendly and mistrustful one. Frequently it is factionalized and just plain nasty, filled with students who don't know how to be supportive, tolerant, or even nice. Conflicts may arise from:

> formation of cliques and scapegoating
>
> intolerance of racial or cultural differences
>
> lack of support from classmates leading to loneliness and isolation
>
> resentment of the accomplishments, possessions, or qualities of others

3. *Poor communication.* Poor communication creates especially fertile ground for conflict. Many conflicts can be attributed to misunderstanding or misperception of the intentions, feelings, needs, or actions of others. Poor communication can also contribute to conflict when students:

> don't know how to express their needs and wishes effectively
>
> have no forum for expressing emotions and needs, or are afraid to do so
>
> cannot listen to others
>
> do not observe carefully

4. *Inappropriate expression of emotion.* All conflicts have an affective component, and how children express their emotions plays an important role in how conflicts develop. Conflicts can escalate when students:

> are out of touch with their feelings
>
> don't know nonaggressive ways to express anger and frustration
>
> suppress emotions
>
> lack self-control

5. *Lack of conflict resolution skills.* Classroom conflicts may escalate when students—and teachers—don't know how to respond creatively

to conflicts. Parents and peer groups often reward violent or very aggressive approaches to conflict, and there are certainly models for this kind of behavior, if only from television. Other factors may affect the acquisition of conflict resolution skills, such as the child's general maturity and stage of moral development.

6. *Misuse of power by the teacher.* It may be disconcerting to think that by misusing your power in the classroom, you can create a whole batch of conflicts all by yourself, but it's true. In the first place, you have a very strong influence on the factors named above. Second, you can contribute to classroom conflict whenever you:

> frustrate a student by placing irrational or impossibly high expectations on him or her
>
> manage a class with a multitude of inflexible rules
>
> continually resort to the authoritarian use of power
>
> establish an atmosphere of fear and mistrust

Did any of those sound familiar? At one time or another, these problems occur in the most well-managed of classrooms. It's when they become part of a way of life in a classroom that they cause real trouble. And that is what this book is about.

There are several beliefs underlying this work. The major one is that adults and children can learn to resolve their conflicts creatively and constructively, in ways that enhance both learning and interpersonal relationships. Another is that teachers are competent, sensitive, and capable of effectively dealing with conflict. This is not a teacher-proof curriculum. In fact, it trusts teachers to make the most important decisions about what will be used in their classrooms, and when. A third belief is that students and teachers deserve practical information and activities. Everything in this book has been tested and retested by myself and by teachers from kindergarten up to and including grade six, in a variety of settings ranging from inner city schools to affluent suburbs to four-room rural schools.

There is an obvious need for people with greater peacemaking skills in a society that is pervaded by violence. Teachers, perhaps more than anyone else, see the effects of this violence on children and their behavior. A classroom atmosphere charged with bad feelings, lack of trust, and unresolved or suppressed conflicts is not conducive to learning. Nor is it an especially pleasant place to teach. But we are in a unique position. We can make a change, and the time to begin is now. For in this age of "back to basics," it is becoming increasingly clear to more and more teachers, parents, and students that we have neglected one of the most basic skills of all.

Chapter 1

Understanding Conflict

Read! And prepare for the coming conflict.
—"Mother" Mary Jones

"Andrew, why did you hit him?"

"He hit me first."

"He says you hit him first."

"I didn't. He hit me first."

"That still doesn't answer my question. Why did you hit him?"

"I'll fight. I won't run away. I'll fight."

"And that's why you hit him?"

"He hit me first."

How many times have you had that kind of conversation? I've had it more times than I care to remember. I was on one side as a child, on the other as a teacher. It is an age-old dialogue, one that reflects the fact that primarily we are taught three ways to deal with conflict situations. They are to:

1. respond aggressively, i.e., physically, verbally, or in some other way to beat our opponent

2. appeal to a higher authority or someone stronger to battle for us

3. ignore the situation

Usually we choose the third option when we can't get anyone to help us and haven't the energy to slug it out, or are afraid we might lose.

We meet with conflict every day, in every way, shape, and form. It is a powerful and pervasive phenomenon. But knowing that doesn't help teachers very much. What does conflict mean to you? Try making a quick list. What are some of the associations, images, and memories that the term *classroom conflict* brings to mind?

1. _____

2. _____

3. _____

4. _____

5. _____

Perhaps you saw images of bloody noses and black eyes. Or a girl left all alone on the playground because no one will play with her. Or groups of black and white students glaring angrily at each other. Or a classroom in chaos. Were all your associations negative?

Now close your eyes for a moment, and try to imagine a classroom with no conflicts at all. How is it?

☐ heavenly   ☐ boring   ☐ impossible to imagine

What is a common conflict in your classroom? _____

_____

_____

What is the most nightmarish conflict in your classroom? _____

_____

_____

What kind of emotional reaction do you have to these or other classroom conflicts?

☐ anger   ☐ fear   ☐ resignation

☐ frustration   ☐ exasperation   ☐ all of the above and more

☐ annoyance   ☐ tears

By now you may be wondering what the point of all this is. It's simple: if we are to understand conflict better, it helps to examine our own experiences, attitudes, and fears before looking at a larger, more abstract picture. Also, these exercises bring out an important point. If you are like most teachers, you tend to see conflict in exclusively negative terms. But a number of important and positive effects has been attributed to conflict, among them:

1. preventing stagnation

2. stimulating creative problem solving

3. engendering personal, organizational, and societal change

4. contributing to self-assessment and skill testing[1]

In other words, without conflict there would be no growth, no learning, no change. Conflict is essential to life.

If you find the idea that conflict is positive hard to swallow, try looking at it this way instead: classroom conflict is either *functional* or *dysfunctional*. Functional conflicts serve a useful purpose. Their results are positive. They may lead to improved classroom relationships, or to more sensible classroom routine, or to better understanding between students. The results of dysfunctional conflicts are negative. They may lead to your having to be more authoritarian, or to some kids feeling victorious while others feel beaten and scapegoated, or to increased violence. In most cases, a given conflict has the potential for being either functional or dysfunctional. What makes it one or the other is not just the conflict itself, but also our response to it.

How Do You Respond to Conflicts?

The following exercises are designed to help you take a closer look at how you respond to classroom conflicts. There are no trick questions and no absolutely right or wrong answers. The purpose of the exercises is not to open your behavior to judgment, but simply to make you more aware of it.

Read the statements below. If a statement describes a response you usually make to classroom conflict, write "3" in the appropriate answer blank below. If it is a response you occasionally make, write "2" in the appropriate blank; and if you rarely or never make that response, write "1."

When there's a classroom conflict, I:

1. tell the kids to knock it off

2. try to make everyone feel at ease

3. help the kids understand each other's point of view

4. separate the kids and keep them away from each other

5. let the principal handle it

6. decide who started it

7. try to find out what the real problem is
8. try to work out a compromise
9. turn it into a joke
10. tell them to stop making such a fuss over nothing
11. make one kid give in and apologize
12. encourage the kids to find alternative solutions
13. help them decide what they can give on
14. try to divert attention from the conflict
15. let the kids fight it out, as long as no one's hurt
16. threaten to send the kids to the principal
17. present the kids some alternatives from which to choose
18. help everyone feel comfortable
19. get everyone busy doing something else
20. tell the kids to settle it on their own time, after school

	I	II	III	IV	V
	1 _____	2 _____	3 _____	4 _____	5 _____
	6 _____	7 _____	8 _____	9 _____	10 _____
	11 _____	12 _____	13 _____	14 _____	15 _____
	16 _____	17 _____	18 _____	19 _____	20 _____
Totals	_____	_____	_____	_____	_____

Now add the numbers in each column. Each column reflects a particular approach and attitude toward classroom conflict. In which column did you score highest? Find the appropriate number below and see if the description corresponds to your perception of your attitudes toward conflict.

I   *The no-nonsense approach.* I don't give in. I try to be fair and honest with the kids, but they need firm guidance in learning what's acceptable behavior and what isn't.

II   *The problem-solving approach.* If there's a conflict, there's a problem. Instead of battling the kids, I try to set up a situation in which we can all solve the problem together. This produces creative ideas and stronger relationships.

III   *The compromising approach.* I listen to the kids and help them listen to each other. Then I help them give a little. We can't all have everything we want. Half a loaf is better than none.

IV   *The smoothing approach.* I like things to stay calm and peaceful whenever possible. Most of the kids' conflicts are relatively unimportant, so I just direct attention to other things.

V *The ignoring approach.* I point out the limits and let the kids work things out for themselves. It's good for them, and they need to learn the consequences of their behavior. There's not a whole lot you can do about conflict situations anyway.

At one time or another, each of these approaches is appropriate. There are times, for instance, when ignoring the conflict is the best response. There are also times, particularly if a child's safety is at stake, when a very firm, no-nonsense stance is necessary, when the problem-solving approach, say, simply won't work.

It is useful to assess our predominant conflict resolution styles because we tend to get stuck on one or two styles and apply them inappropriately. Our emphasis, however, is not on judging our behavior but rather on increasing our repertoire of peacemaking skills and learning how and when to apply them most effectively. This depends in part on the type of conflict that occurs.

Types of Conflict

In a classroom—and most other situations as well—conflicts are usually of three types: conflicts over resources, conflict of needs, and conflicts of values.

Conflicts over resources occur when two or more people want something that is in short supply, e.g., the ball, the toy trucks, the attention of the teacher, the job of clapping erasers, the friendship of the new kid. These conflicts are often the easiest to resolve.

Children have, of course, many needs, including needs for power, friendship and affiliation, self-esteem, and achievement. Any of these can conflict with the needs of someone else in the class, sometimes overtly, sometimes very subtly. Conflicts of needs are trickier to resolve than conflicts over resources, largely because the reasons for them are less distinct.

When values, those beliefs we hold most dear, clash, the conflict is the most difficult type of all to resolve. When our values are challenged, we often feel that our whole sense of self is threatened, and we cling to our position with a tenacity that other types of conflict don't inspire. Incidentally, conflicts of values are not limited to religious, political, and other beliefs. Goal conflicts are also value conflicts. We all pursue goals; the degree to which we pursue any given goal reflects the value we place on it. Some goals are more important to us than others. When goals conflict, resolution is difficult when both (or all) the participants highly value the conflicting goals.

The distinctions between these three types of conflict are sometimes difficult to draw. For example, say that two girls in a ball game are arguing over whose turn it is to pitch. Are they expressing conflicting needs for power, or are they contending for a limited resource, i.e., the right to pitch? Both, probably. Labeling a conflict simply helps you choose a means of resolving it. It's a good idea to start by taking the conflict at face value—in this case, a conflict of resources—and then you can revise your assessment if necessary as you define the problem.

Just as it is useful to be able to label the type of conflict, it also helps to know that most conflicts, large or small, interpersonal or international, follow pretty much the same pattern. To get a good conflict going, you need:[2]

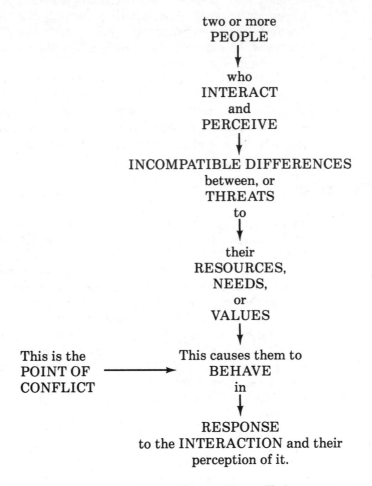

two or more
PEOPLE

↓

who
INTERACT
and
PERCEIVE

↓

INCOMPATIBLE DIFFERENCES
between, or
THREATS
to

↓

their
RESOURCES,
NEEDS,
or
VALUES

↓

This is the   This causes them to
POINT OF   ———————→   BEHAVE
CONFLICT   in

↓

RESPONSE
to the INTERACTION and their
perception of it.

The conflict will then

ESCALATE   **or**   DE-ESCALATE

The conflict will ESCALATE if:

1.   there is an increase in exposed emotion, e.g., anger, frustration
2.   there is an increase in perceived threat
3.   more people get involved, choosing up sides
4.   the children were not friends prior to the conflict
5.   the children have few peacemaking skills at their disposal

The conflict will DE-ESCALATE if:

1.   attention is focused on the problem, not on the participants
2.   there is a decrease in exposed emotion and perceived threat
3.   the children were friends prior to the conflict
4.   they know how to make peace, or have someone to help them do so

All of this can take place in the space of three minutes, or three months, depending on the specific conflict.

De-escalation cools the conflict, keeping it from spreading and becoming more violent. At its best, conflict resolution is a de-escalation of a conflict that channels it along functional rather than dysfunctional lines.

This is very different from the aggressive or passive, fight-or-flight responses to conflict I discussed at the beginning of the chapter, i.e., attack, appeal to a third party, or ignoring the situation. The difficulty with these aggressive or passive alternatives is that they are not, after all, particularly effective ways of handling conflicts. They tend to be accompanied by physical or emotional hurt, humiliation, and suppressed anger. They also tend not to solve problems. Our awareness of the ineffectiveness of the aggressive or passive responses frequently leaves us at the mercy of a conflict, feeling overwhelmed by it and powerless to respond effectively. Before long, we start believing that there is no way to resolve conflicts—"either the other person wins, or I win, period"—and we are locked into a behavior pattern with no apparent way out.

We need not be trapped this way. Between aggression and inaction is a whole range of responses we haven't discovered. That's all creative conflict resolution is—looking for constructive alternatives and acting on them. Losing and winning, traditionally defined, are not our only options.

Different Approaches to Conflict

Let's take a minute to examine this business of winning. Winning in a conflict situation means getting what you need (or want) in that situation. It may or may not have anything to do with besting your opponent.

For example:

Ms. Evans: I told you the projects were due Friday, and that's final.

Janine: To do a good job, I've got to have more time!

Here is a conflict of needs. Ms. Evans needs to feel that her authority is respected. Janine needs to feel she has done a competent job. It looks as though either Ms. Evans will win, or Janine. But if we chart the alternatives, we can see other possibilities. Certainly, either Ms. Evans or Janine might win, and the other lose. They could, however, also both win or both lose. Clearly, the happiest resolution would be one in which they both win.[3]

	Ms. Evans gets what she needs	Ms. Evans doesn't get what she needs
Janine gets what she needs	win-win	win-lose
Janine doesn't get what she needs	win-lose	lose-lose

Approaching a conflict as if both parties could win completely changes our orientation toward conflict resolution. Attention shifts away from the participants and onto their problem and how to solve it.

Just how you define the problem is very important, for it establishes your orientation toward a win-win resolution. To recognize and define the conflict clearly involve gathering facts about the situation and opening communication so that perceptions about what is happening can be aired and clarified. The most important part of clarifying the situation is attempting to discover the real needs of each person in the conflict. For example:

Rachel: I *like* to make towers out of blocks and knock them over with my truck.

Adam: I'm trying to read, and the noise bothers me.

The problem here may appear to be how to keep Rachel from disturbing Adam, or possibly vice versa. The difficulty with that definition of the problem, however, is that it focuses on the participants and sets up a win-lose situation. If the problem is thus defined, Adam will probably get what he wants: a particular solution is built into the definition, which is cast in terms of possible resolutions rather than in terms of needs.

What do Adam and Rachel really need, then? They may not be able to tell you, so you will have to do some probing and some assuming. In this instance, what they really need is space in which to pursue their activities freely. The problem is how to find such space. This kind of focus makes a win-win solution possible.

In the case of Ms. Evans and Janine, there is presumably a shared desire that the highest quality learning take place via Janine's independent project. The problem, then, is how best to facilitate this high-quality learning.

Unfortunately, you might not be able to get Ms. Evans and Janine to agree that this statement of the problem would in fact lead to satisfaction of their needs. Their problem could instead be stated: how can Janine get her project done to her satisfaction without Ms. Evans feeling that her authority is being ignored? This is a fairly complex statement, to be sure, but still one that points toward a win-win solution. We are saying that both should have their needs satisfied.

Identifying problems in terms of needs is not easy. We tend to promote solutions in our definitions of problems. Also, children are often unable to state their needs clearly. When this happens, ask yourself what the children are doing and what they hope to accomplish by it. When you think you've got a fair idea of the needs of each child in the situation, check your definition of the problem with them. For the resolution to get anywhere, all parties must agree on the definition of their problem.

Obviously, you can't always end up with a win-win solution. Sometimes you end up with a win-lose or even a lose-lose resolution. (Incidentally, compromise can be considered a lose-lose resolution because each party gives up something.) However, there is a world of difference between ending up with a win and a loss and starting out with a win-lose orientation.

I do not mean to imply that the process of creative conflict resolution is either easy or guaranteed. It isn't. Nor am I saying that all conflicts can be tidily resolved. They cannot. But they can be confronted in ways that try to meet the needs of all involved.

Once you get going, I think you and your students will discover between violence and inaction a whole range of effective and satisfying responses to that ancient accusation, "He started it!"

Notes

1. Alan C. Filley, *Interpersonal Conflict Resolution* (Glenview, Ill.: Scott, Foresman and Co., 1975), pp. 4–7.
2. Morton Deutsch, *The Resolution of Conflict* (New Haven: Yale University Press, 1973), pp. 5–8, 350–353.
3. Filley, *Interpersonal Conflict Resolution*, pp. 21–30.

Chapter 2

Resolving Student vs. Student Conflicts

There is probably no elementary school in the country that does not have a rule against fights of the punching, kicking, hitting variety. On the other hand, there is probably no elementary school in the country that does not have fights. When we tell children not to fight without giving them alternative ways to settle disputes, they fight.

In contrast to violent conflict is the quieter—and more common—conflict that one of my students once called the fester fight. When I asked what she meant, she explained, "Nobody hits; nobody does nothing. They just sit and *fester* for a long, long time." In this essentially passive approach to conflict, the kids are once again trapped without an alternative.

The conflict resolution techniques discussed in this chapter can help you show kids that there are different ways to settle disputes. These techniques have worked for me and for the teachers who have attended my workshops. The illustrative examples come from teachers who work in a variety of settings.

Choosing a Conflict Resolution Technique

To choose a conflict resolution technique, consider four things:

1. *Who's involved?* How many, how old, how mature, and how angry are they? What are their needs? (You will go into this in greater detail when you define the problem.)

2. *Is the time right?* Do you have enough time to work things out now, or should you wait? Do the participants need to cool off first? Is it too soon to talk things out?

3. *How appropriate is a particular resolution technique?* Is this a simple dispute over resources, or a complex conflict of values? What is the problem? Will this technique help solve the problem? Is the technique so sophisticated that the kids need training in it first?

4. *Should the resolution be public or private?* Would the participants be embarrassed by a public resolution? Would the class benefit from seeing this conflict resolved? Could they help with the resolution? Do you have the time to resolve it publicly?

A conflict resolution technique simply provides a safe, structured way to air grievances, feelings, and differences of opinion so that a conflict can serve a useful purpose. The descriptions of techniques that follow are not written in stone. You know your classroom; you know your students. If the techniques need adapting to your situation, please adapt them. The world needs all the creative conflict resolution techniques it can get!

Fights

The simplest way to deal with a fight is to:

1. break it up
2. cool it off
3. work it out

Breaking up a fight isn't always easy. Unfortunately, I can give you no magic formula for doing it, only a few suggestions. (Fortunately, in most cases, the mere presence of a teacher is enough to stop a fight.)

If you are going to separate two fighters, first be sure you can do it. This may sound like an idiot's rule, but if the fighters are bigger than you, or so out of control that they are flailing wildly, not only you may fail to break it up, you may get badly hurt in the bargain. Also, if you don't have help, you will probably be able to restrain only one of the fighters, leaving him or her vulnerable to attack. This is not going to win you any points as a peacemaker. It is far better to round up a few strong kids to help hold back the fighters; or, if you must, let the fight run its course. In a real emergency, grabbing the kids by the hair will usually stop a fight right away. That is, however, an extreme (and violent) tactic.

Think of a fight as a concentration of physical and emotional energy. Anything you can do to divert this energy will help cool the situation. For example, if you are present just as a fight is beginning, try distracting the participants: "Hey, who lost this dollar?" Or try getting very close to the fighters and shouting loudly.

When kids fight, there are usually spectators. Try to get them to leave, or at least to sit down and stare silently. Two fighters soon feel like fools if they are in the middle of a group of silent, staring people. Or, if you can, get everyone either to chant ("Stop fighting, stop fighting") or to sing (the jollier the better). I once saw a teacher stop a street fight involving several of her students by having the rest of the class circle the fight with hands joined, singing "Ring around the Rosy." The very ridiculousness of the action is a clue to its effectiveness. She established a situation in which fighting became incongruous.

Many of these suggestions require the cooperation of the class. Prior training is essential here, or you are likely to find yourself trying to deal with a fight as the class looks at you as if you had gone crazy. But (who knows?) maybe that will be enough to stop a fight.

Described below are techniques for cooling off and working out conflicts. You will notice that all of these techniques involve you, usually in the role of mediator. This is not to imply that your students should remain dependent on you to resolve their conflicts. One of the goals of creative conflict resolution is to get kids resolving their own conflicts, nonviolently. This takes thorough training, however, of the kind described in chapter four. Use the techniques described here until your students are more independent as peacemakers.

Cooling Off

Grades K–6

Procedure:

When a conflict becomes so volatile that violence breaks out, the participants are not likely to be able to work things out nonviolently until some of the emotion exposed in the conflict has dissipated. There are several ways to calm antagonists:

1. Establish cool-off corners. These are areas where fighters are sent not to be punished but to calm down. Obviously, you need separate corners for each fighter. When they feel they have cooled off, they may leave the corners.

2. Get the kids to try deep breathing. Have them take slow, deep breaths while you count to ten and then back to one again.

3. Try having the participants sit silently for a few minutes.

(More cooling-off suggestions are given in chapter six.)

Cooling off de-escalates a conflict; it doesn't resolve it. The technical name for it is postponing. Sometimes, however, two fighters cool down to find that they would just as soon skip the whole thing. In this case, you should check to see that no hard feelings remain, and then let it go.

Example:

Jackie and Peter were fighting on the playground when a teacher-aide separated them. When she tried to determine the problem, she couldn't understand a word that was being said for the tears and shouting. Having the boys sit silently and breathe deeply for a couple of minutes, she quickly calmed things down to a point where the problem could be tackled.

Mediation

Grades K–6

Procedure:

Most of the conflict resolution you practice between children will be mediation. It is a way of helping people work out their differences in the presence of a calm, nonpartisan observer who keeps everything fair. Fairness is very important to children; you should try to stay as impartial as possible.

Mediating takes time, and you should try to give it the time it deserves. The following procedure is an effective one:

1. Tell the children that each of them will have an opportunity to give his or her side of the story without interruption.

2. As each child talks, have him or her first tell what the problem was and then what happened during the conflict.

3. If the problem still exists, help the participants to develop some possible solutions and to choose one to implement.

4. If the problem no longer exists, ask the participants if there might have been more effective ways to solve the problem than the one they chose.

Example:

Carol, a popular fifth grader, has accused Alicia, who is not well liked, of stealing her lunch money. She has done this loudly and publicly. The teacher, Edna Green, takes the girls aside and explains the mediating process.

EG: Carol, suppose you start. What's the problem?

C: She took my lunch money.

EG: Your lunch money is gone, and you suspect that she took it.

C: Yeah.

EG: Why do you suspect her?

C: She had to stay in at recess. Susie walked by the door and saw her at my desk. Everyone knows she steals.

EG: No, I don't know that. What we're trying to do is find your money. Do you have anything else to say?

C: No.

EG: Alicia, what do you have to say?

A: Nothing. I didn't take her money.

EG: Were you at her desk?

A: Yes, but only because when I walked by I bumped it, and some papers fell out, and I put them back. That's all.

EG: Okay, Carol, you say she took your money when she was at your desk. Alicia, you say you were putting papers back. What do we do now?

C: Search her desk.

A: Search *her* desk.

EG: Have you looked through your desk carefully, Carol?

C: I don't have to. The money was at the front.

EG: Why don't you look once more?

[*Carol does so, and returns having found the money.*]

EG: Well, what do we do now?

C: I'm sorry, Alicia.

A: That's okay.

EG: Wait a minute. You accused her in front of the class.

C: I guess I should tell the class I was wrong.

A: She doesn't have to.

C: I will. I was wrong.

EG: When you're wrong, it's best to admit it and get it over. Shake hands, and let's go back.

This was a delicate problem that fortunately turned out to be one not of theft but of false accusation. Edna strictly maintained her impartiality and from the beginning defined the problem in a way that focused on the problem itself, not Alicia's presumed guilt or innocence. Clearly, this is a class in which more community should be built so that such scapegoating does not recur.

Reflective Listening

Grades K–6   **Procedure:**

Reflective or active listening is a way of paraphrasing, reflecting back to the speaker what he or she has said. This gives the speaker an opportunity to affirm or correct your perception. It is a very useful mediation technique.

Reflective listening is not a conflict resolution technique per se; it is known in conflict resolution circles as a perception-clarifying device. It allows you to identify more clearly what people think and feel about a conflict situation. Sometimes this is sufficient to resolve the conflict. At other times, it may just help you to state the problem clearly.

1. You might reflect by using such phrases as "Sounds like ———;" "In other words, ———;" or "You're saying ———."

2. When you paraphrase, try to reflect the emotional as well as factual content. The following formula is useful for getting the knack: "Sounds like you feel ——— because ———." If this formula seems stilted and unnatural, don't worry. You will find that you soon incorporate it by adapting it to your natural speech patterns.

Reflective listening tends to slow down interaction. Bear in mind that it is intended to clarify situations, not slow them maddeningly. Use it selectively.

Example:

Janet Graham is mediating between Raphael and Annie, two sixth graders who are trying to work jointly on a project.

A: He's not doing any of the work. I have to do everything.

JG: You feel you have to do most of the work because Raphael's not contributing to the project.

A: Right. When we look things up, he wastes time looking at stuff that doesn't have anything to do with the project.

JG: You want to work efficiently.

A: Yeah.

R: I get ideas for our project by looking at other things. You're so bossy I never get a chance to say what my ideas are.

JG: You feel you don't have a chance to share your ideas because Annie doesn't give you time to develop and share them.

R: Yeah. I work different from her.

JG: I'm beginning to see the problem here. Annie wants to work quickly and efficiently but not get stuck doing everything. Raphael wants to take more time and have his ideas listened to. Does that sound right?

A&R: Yes.

JG: I think we're ready to come up with a solution now.

Some important points about this conflict have been clarified by the use of reflective listening. Notice that Janet did not impose her own opinion until she was able to state the problem to the satisfaction of both parties.

Smoothing

Grades K–6

Procedure:

Smoothing is simply glossing over a conflict. There are occasions on which this is the best thing to do. You don't always have time to work through a conflict; and, frankly, some conflicts are too ephemeral to worry about.

There are problems with it, however. For one, it is used entirely too often. Don't let the name fool you. Smoothing is really a classy name for avoiding conflict. It is not really a conflict resolution technique in that nothing is resolved or even confronted. In addition, a conflict that may not seem important to you may be very important to the children involved. Smooth conflicts only when you must.

Example:

The second grade is lining up for lunch. Andrew complains to teacher Mel Power.

A: All the kids keep cutting in front of me in line.

MP: They get ahead of you in line, and you think that's not fair.

A: Yes.

MP: Are you really bothered by it?

A: No, I guess not.

MP: Then let's not worry about it right now. Would that be okay?

A: Yes.

Mel combined smoothing with reflective listening; he smoothed this situation without ignoring the child's needs or feelings. A useful follow-up would be to have the class establish a policy on line cutting.

Storytelling

Grades K–3

Procedure:

The storytelling technique helps young children distance themselves from a conflict so they can discuss their behavior. It is especially good for public conflict resolution.

1. Tell the story of the conflict situation using a "Once upon a time" format. (Change the names of the participants if you think that's important. My experience has been that doing so often reduces the story to a guessing game.)

2. When the story reaches the point of conflict, stop and ask the class for suggestions on how to resolve it.

3. Incorporate one of the suggestions into the story, and bring it to its conclusion.

4. Ask the real participants if this would in fact meet their needs and if it is something they might try the next time they have a problem.

This technique can be adapted for mediating conflicts between older students. Have them tell the story of the conflict in the third person, as if they were neutral observers. Again, this can provide just enough distance for the kids to analyze the situation and their behavior without feeling threatened.

Example:

A problem occurred in Pat Rosen's kindergarten. She brought it before the class.

PR: Once upon a time, Eleanor and Amy were playing with Matchbox cars. Eleanor wanted to use the fire truck at the same time Amy did. They both started to get mad and yell at each other. What could they do?

1:   Share?

PR: They don't want to share. They both want to play with it now.

2:   You could tell them they both have to share.

PR:	I'm busy. They have to solve this themselves.
3:	They could throw the cars around.
PR:	They tried that. It didn't work.
4:	Take turns.
PR:	How?
4:	I don't know. Flip a coin?
PR:	Well, you know, that's just what they did. Eleanor got to play with it first; then Amy got a turn. Do you think that would work with the real Amy and Eleanor?
E&A:	Yes.
PR:	How do you think they played then? They played happily ever after.

Pat did not let the children get away with any vague answers, such as a simple "Share." Notice how she insisted that they spell out how the sharing would take place, i.e., taking turns in an order decided by flipping a coin. Requiring this sort of specificity helps prevent give-the-teacher-what-she-wants-to-hear responses. The very specific answer is more likely to affect behavior in the long run.

Time Out

Grades K–6

Procedure:

This technique is useful for weaning children from their dependence on you for resolving all their conflicts.

1. When students bring you a conflict, send them to a quiet spot in the room. Give them three minutes to work out the problem without your help.

2. After three minutes, see if they have worked out a resolution. If not, proceed as if you were hearing about the conflict for the first time.

3. If they worked out a resolution, praise them and ask what it is.

Example:

Tisha and Dannielle are two third graders in Jeri Foley's class. They are in charge of planning a surprise party for a student who is moving but can't agree on what they want to do. They have brought their dispute to Jeri. She says, "It seems to me that you two have got a lot of work to do and need to get going. Why don't you go over behind the bookshelf for three minutes and try to work out a way to choose an idea? Don't choose now. Try to come up with a plan for choosing. I'll time you, and if you haven't worked anything out after three minutes, I'll help you."

The girls buzzed in the corner for three minutes and then announced that they had worked out an arrangement: for every idea of Dannielle's they used, they would also use one of Tisha's.

Jeri used the time out technique to encourage the girls to solve the problem themselves. In this instance, she sent them away with a very specific charge. You don't need to be so specific; a simple "Try to work something out" is usually sufficient.

This is obviously not a technique to use when tempers are really flaring and the kids could easily start fighting all over again. It is one to use when things are relatively calm and you think the participants are ready to go it alone.

Fight Forms

Grades 2–6

Procedure:

The fight form (see Appendix) is a way of getting kids to look carefully at a conflict they are in. I use filling them out as one of the consequences of the no-fighting rule in my classroom (see chapter three).

1. When the kids have calmed down from their fight, point out the ineffectiveness of fighting. Do not ask for an explanation; instead, give them a fight form to fill out.

2. When the forms are completed, read them over with the participants. Discuss not how or why the conflict developed, but what the students have said they will do in such a situation in the future. Ask, "Will this action solve the problem better than fighting?"

3. Or have the fighters exchange papers when they are finished and write their reactions to each other's accounts.

Example:

Name   Jeffrey

Fight Form

With whom did you fight? Keith and Janet

What was the problem? We were supposed to work together and they wouldn't listen to my ideas.

Why did you start fighting? (Give two reasons.) Keith and Janet wouldn't listen, and Janet said my ideas were dumb. Keith said they were dumb too.

Why did the other person fight with you? Keith said don't hit Janet.

Did fighting solve the problem? No

What are three things you might try if this happens again?
1. I could come tell you.
2. I could go along with their ideas.
3. I could say please listen.

Is there anything you would like to say to the person you fought with? Tell them they have to listen to people if they work in groups.

This fight form gave me a clear idea of how to proceed toward a resolution. It also showed me that some of my kids needed work in specific cooperation skills.

🍎 Filling out the fight form also gives the participants a chance to cool off before confronting each other.

Fight Fair Method[1]

Grades 2–6

Procedure:

This adaptation of Bach and Wyden's Fight Fair Method provides older elementary students with a broad but effective framework for resolving differences. The rules for each participant are:

1. State the facts as calmly as possible. Refer only to the present situation, not the past or future.

2. Express how you feel. Talk about your feelings without making negative remarks about the other person.

3. Find out what you can do about the situation. Try to think of a solution that will satisfy all the participants.

This technique takes some practice, and role playing can provide it. Until the kids are accustomed to using the technique, you should be on hand as a mediator. It helps to post the procedure as a reminder of the steps.

Example:

Fran, a fifth grader, has worked long and hard on a plaster of paris sculpture. Alice, without asking, picked it up and was taking a look at it when it fell and smashed. Fran is furious and vows to destroy something of Alice's. As Peter Carr enters the room, Fran is headed for Alice's desk, with Alice desperately trying to block her way. He separates the girls, sits them down, and insists that they fight fair.

PC: Okay, facts first.

F: She broke my art project.

PC: How?

F: She picked it up after I told everyone not to touch it, and she dropped it.

PC: Did you?

A: Yes, but it was an accident. Then she said she'd break something of mine.

PC: What?

A: I don't know. Whatever she could find.

PC: How do you feel right now, Fran?

F: Really, really mad. I hate her.

PC: Any other feelings?

F: I worked hard on that project. I guess I'm a little sad, too.

PC: Alice?

A: Well, I'm mad at her, too.

PC: Anything else?

A: I feel a little sorry, too.

F: That doesn't help put my project back together.

PC: What would help you feel better?

F: She could start by saying she's sorry.

PC: What about you, Alice?

A: I'll say I'm sorry because I was wrong. But it was an accident. She shouldn't wreck anything of mine. I only picked it up because I liked it.

PC: Fran?

F: Okay. But I'll have to start all over again. She has to promise not to touch the new one.

A: All right.

Peter maintained his neutrality throughout this interchange by adhering to the Fight Fair rules. Although in this case it wasn't necessary, it is often helpful to summarize the fact-finding portion of the procedure with a clear definition of the problem.

Role Playing

Grades 3–6

Procedure:

Role playing as a conflict resolution technique involves reenacting a conflict situation to help students gain new understanding of their behavior.

1. Describe the conflict situation, giving time, place, and background. Define the roles to be played; and ask the participants to play the roles, or use volunteers.

2. Have the players act out the conflict. If they get stuck, help them along with leading questions. Keep it short.

3. Freeze the role play at the point of conflict. Ask the audience for suggestions as to what could be done next. The players then incorporate one of these into the role play and wind it up.

4. Always discuss the role play when it is finished. How could the conflict have been prevented? How did the characters feel in the situation? Was it a satisfactory solution? What other solutions might have worked?

Before you begin using role play as a conflict resolution technique, give the kids some practice with hypothetical situations. These are less threatening than actual conflict situations. Be sensitive, too, to the fact that not all students like to participate in role play. The technique need not always be used for public resolutions, either. It works just as well privately, although you need to be on hand to guide it.

🍎 Role play can be used with younger children, with varying degrees of success. The problem is that young children lack the maturity necessary to disassociate themselves from the roles they play. It's sometimes worth a try, however. (See also Problem Puppets, below.)

Example:
Tommy and Dewight are in charge of setting up a display for the school lobby. Their theme is Contributions of Black Americans, but they cannot agree on what to display or on how to set up the display. They have arrived at a sullen stalemate.

Ms. Kelly asked them to describe the problem to her and then asked if they'd be willing to present it to the class as a role play. They agreed, and are just arriving at the point of conflict.

T: You want all these people no one ever heard of, like your grandmother!

D: And you just want famous people everyone already knows!

Ms. K: Freeze! Can anyone suggest how Tommy and Dewight can get past this stalemate?

1:   Compromise.

Ms. K: How?

1:   Make lists of people, and each choose the five they want.

2:   Put names on papers, and pull them from a hat.

3:   No, don't compromise. Have them make lists and see if they agree on any names.

4:   Have the class pick the names.

T&D: No!

Ms. K: Do any of these ideas excite you?

T: I'd be willing to pick five names.

D: Me too.

Ms. K: Okay. Suppose you two try that and see how it goes. If it doesn't work, the class can always come up with something else.

This is an example of problem solving with role play. In this instance, it wasn't necessary to play the roles through to the point of resolution. For even so mild a conflict as this, Ms. Kelly made sure to obtain the participants' permission before presenting the problem to the class. You can tell from the ease and quality of responses that this class is accustomed to role play. A nice touch was Ms. Kelly's assurance that the class would be available to provide further assistance if needed.

Role Reversals

Grades 3–6

Procedure:
Role reversals can be a dramatic way to help solve stubborn conflicts.

1.   Establish the role play as above. Try to use the participants in the original conflict as players.

2. Once the role play has started, freeze it, and have the participants change roles and replay it, so that they are, in effect, arguing against themselves.

3. Stop the role play after the players have gotten the feel of the other person's point of view, in a minute or so. Discuss the role play as above, and see if any new light is shed on the subject.

Example:

At Duncan Elementary School, the two fourth grades had enough money to take one field trip together. One class had studied astronomy and wanted to go to the planetarium. The other class wanted to visit a nature center. The disagreement was creating problems between classes.

The teachers decided to try role reversals. They explained both sides of the conflict to the combined classes. Then they asked for volunteers to participate in a hassle line, which is a kind of mass role play (see chapter four). Almost everyone volunteered. The classes formed two lines, with each student facing a partner from the other class.

For one minute, the students in one fourth grade tried to convince their partners to go to the planetarium. Then the other class got one minute to argue for the nature center. Then the two classes switched roles, and each class took one minute to argue the opposite viewpoint. When all the noise and confusion died down, the students understood both sides of the conflict better than they possibly could have before.

The teachers then used a problem-solving technique to get the classes to choose a mutually satisfactory field trip.

The Problem Puppets[2]

Grades K-2

Materials: puppets

Procedure:

The problem puppets are used as role players. Puppet players provide young children enough distance from a conflict to discuss their own behavior without feeling threatened.

1. Have several puppets available, and explain their use to the children: "These are the problem puppets, and they exist to help solve problems." I always made a big deal of the problem puppets. They lived in a specially marked shoe box. I had the children name them, and each puppet was marked with a large P.

2. When there is a conflict, use the puppets to reenact the situation, either before a group or privately. Unless you have older children who are experienced with puppets, you will probably have to work the puppets yourself.

3. Freeze the puppet role play at the point of conflict. Solicit suggestions on ways to solve the problem. Incorporate one of these suggestions, and finish the role play.

4. Do this with several different suggestions if you have time. Include one or two that won't work. This helps children learn to think through the consequences of their suggestions.

5. When you have incorporated a solution that seems to work, ask the participants if that is a solution satisfactory to them. If it is, the conflict is resolved, and the problem puppets can be temporarily retired.

Example:

Carolyn and Allen were bickering about who had saved a place on the rug for their kindergarten teacher to sit. Their teacher, Tim Hall—you remember him—went to the shoebox that housed the problem puppets and took two of them out. Sitting with the class, he reenacted the situation and then asked for solutions.

Unfortunately, none of the suggestions yielded a satisfactory solution, and the problem persisted, with different participants, for a week. Then one day someone suggested that the puppets make saving a seat for Mr. Hall one of the jobs on the job chart. Everyone agreed that this just might be the answer. One of the puppets pointed out that sometimes problems take a while to solve.

I have found when using the problem puppets that it is not necessary to change the names of the conflicting parties. For one thing, everyone probably knows who they are; and, for another, the children usually do not mind being named. In fact, they are often delighted.

3R Strategy[3]

Grades 4–6

Procedure:

This is a highly structured technique, particularly useful in cases of long-standing disagreement and dislike. There are three steps: resentment, request, and recognition.

1. *Resentment.* Each party states what he or she dislikes about the other and outlines everything done to cause the resentment.

2. *Request.* Each party tells the other what to do to solve the problem.

3. *Recognition.* Both parties negotiate which requests they would be willing to meet. Finally, the session ends with each party stating what qualities they like or find admirable in each other.

As you may have gathered, the 3R strategy is a heavy-duty one. It requires time, and a firm mediator who can keep all the exposed emotion under control. It is very useful for clearing the air when two students have built up a lot of resentment toward one another. However, it goes over the heads of some students, so you will have to use your judgment and discretion.

Example:

During the sixth grade basketball game, Dana made a pejorative remark about Errol's mother, and a fight broke out between them. The two boys were frequently in conflict, both in class and out. Peggy Anderson, tired of the constant bickering, decided to use the 3R strategy. She arranged a meeting with the boys after school one day and explained the procedure they would use. She made it very clear that each would get his turn and that they would follow the 3R procedure strictly.

Adapted by permission of A&W Publishers, Inc. from *Developing Effective Classroom Groups* by Gene Stanford. Copyright © 1977, Hart Publishing Company, Inc.

Dana said that he resented the remarks Errol made about his lack of height and lack of basketball-playing ability. He also resented the nasty remarks that Errol frequently made in class. Errol said that he resented the slurs on his mother, the fact that Dana always ruined the basketball games, and the way Dana always acted like Mr. Cool.

PA: What do you mean?

E: You know. He thinks he's so smart and best at everything.

D: I do not!

PA: Wait—we're just talking about what each of you resents; we're not wasting time denying anything. Any other resentments? Okay, let's start with requests.

E: I want him to apologize for what he said about my mother.

PA: Anything else?

E: Stop acting so big.

PA: How?

E: Well . . . stop telling everyone how much his clothes cost and what grades he got and stuff.

PA: Anything else?

E: No.

PA: What about you, Dana?

D: I don't like it when people pick on me. He should shut up about my being short.

PA: Is that it?

D: If he thinks I lose the games, he should give me lessons.

PA: Which will you agree to, Errol?

E: I'm not giving him any lessons!

PA: But what *will* you do?

E: Oh, I'll get off his back about lousing up the games and being short. He can't help it.

D: Promise?

E: Yeah, I promise. What will you do?

D: I'm sorry about what I said about your mother. I don't think I brag a lot, but I'll try not to.

PA: Would each of you think of something that you like about the other? Errol?

E: You are smart. And even though you're not good at sports, you keep trying. That's good, I guess.

D: You're real good at sports. And sometimes you say stuff that makes me laugh.

Dana and Errol never became good friends, but their bickering did stop, and so the classroom climate improved.

This is another situation in which playing strictly by the rules of the technique allowed the participants to air their grievances and feel safe in doing so. Notice that Peggy kept things moving right along and did not allow digressions or vaguely worded statements. By keeping everything very matter-of-fact, she gave the boys something concrete with which to work.

Notes

1. "Fight Fair" Method in THE INTIMATE ENEMY by Dr. George R. Bach and Peter Wyden. Copyright © 1968, 1969 by George R. Bach and Peter Wyden. Adapted by permission of William Morrow & Company.
2. I learned this technique from Kathy Allen.
3. Adapted by permission of A&W Publishers, Inc. from *Developing Effective Classroom Groups* by Gene Stanford. Copyright© 1977, Hart Publishing Co., Inc.

Chapter 3

Resolving Student vs. Teacher Conflicts

Delicious Banana is here to say
That bananas taste good in a certain way;
Just peel a banana and throw it on the floor,
And watch your teacher slide out the door.
—Anonymous

I heard that rhyme on the playground not long ago. What interested me about it was that I chanted the same rhyme some twenty-odd years ago. In the folk culture of children, students and teachers are natural enemies. Have you ever watched children play school? The vehemence with which most children play the role of teacher is startling.

Now, under ordinary circumstances, most students do not harbor ambivalence toward a particular teacher, but rather toward teachers as a group. They are reacting to a role, not an individual. This seems rather odd since, logically, teachers and students should be natural allies, not enemies. A closer look at student vs. teacher conflicts shows why.

Most teacher-student clashes are conflicts of either needs or values; rarely are they conflicts over resources. When a student blows up at his or her teacher, most likely there is a conflict of needs. The child's need to express anger conflicts with the teacher's need to be in control of the class. As for value conflicts between teachers and students, they frequently have less to do with religious, political, or other beliefs than with goals. All of us have goals in our classrooms, from teaching students to be good citizens to having students complete all homework assignments. Knowingly or unknowingly, we assign values to these goals. Goals we deem very important are frequently not so important to the kids, and conflict results. For example, when a student repeatedly fails to hand in homework, there is most probably a conflict between the high value the teacher places on the goal of having students complete all assignments and the low value the student places on doing schoolwork.

As if all this were not enough, there is one more crucial factor—power. All people have a need for power over their lives; in classrooms, however, teachers hold virtually all the power. Teacher vs. student conflicts become very complicated because of this unequal relationship. There are few situations in which one person is granted so much power over a group of people involuntarily gathered together, but society gives teachers this power. Parents give us this power. Even children acknowledge the seeming necessity of this power relationship, although they bridle against it, especially if it is abused.

Teachers, however, are often uncomfortable with their power and seldom examine or even acknowledge it. After all, few of us want to be dictators, no matter how benevolent. This unwillingness to examine power relationships is unfortunate because it leads to abuses of power that exacerbate classroom conflict. The power relationship between students and teachers can legitimately be questioned, but not appropriately here. It is more useful at this point to accept and examine our power in the classroom and learn to use it more constructively.

Power Games Teachers Play

There are many reasons why teachers abuse their power, and we'll get to them. First, let's look at some of the ways they abuse power. The cartoons on the next page show teachers playing four power games. There are numerous other power games teachers can and do play. Most of them have these elements in common:

1. Power is used capriciously.
2. The student's lack of power is flaunted.
3. Control is based on fear rather than reason, caring, or any of a number of other positive forces.

Why do teachers play these games? Frequently it is because they confuse authority with authoritarianism. Exerting authority in a classroom involves establishing a learning environment, maintaining order, and eliciting the best from each student. That is what we are paid to do. Authoritarianism, on the other hand, amounts to demanding blind, unquestioning obedience to authority—and there are several reasons to avoid it.

Perhaps the most important reason is an ethical one. If students are to learn self-control and how to use their own power responsibly, they must see someone model the constructive, responsible use of power.

Game 1:

"Because I said so, that's why."

Game 2:

"I don't want to hear about it. Our schedule says it's time for math, and we have to follow our schedule. You'll find in life that . . ."

Game 3:

"Because of the actions of one, we all suffer."

Game 4:

"Thank you, Timmy, for yet another brilliant, insightful, and completely wrong answer."

In practical terms, authoritarian classroom management often backfires. It appears to be very effective because it is quick and gets obvious results. But it deals only with superficialities; and although it may quash open teacher vs. student conflicts, the resentment and hostility that build up in students because of this misuse of power can channel the conflict into other, equally destructive modes.

I'm certainly not suggesting that a classroom in chaos is our aim. There are limits to the amount of conflict any teacher can handle or allow. In addition, years of schooling have made some students dependent on authoritarian teachers because they have learned no self-control. These students must be weaned gradually from authoritarianism.

What's the Problem?
Understanding Goals and Needs

One reason power gets abused in classrooms is that teachers often overreact to student vs. teacher conflicts. They see any such conflict as a threat to their power. This is not necessarily true. We need to define conflicts more carefully than that if we are to resolve them successfully. To do this, let's look at goals and needs.

Goals

Most of your behavior in the classroom is goal-directed, i.e., you are trying to get something accomplished. Your goals can be very broad, as in teaching children to accept responsibility, or very specific, as in having each child memorize the multiplication tables. Broad or specific, each of your goals is probably either academic, affective, or procedural. Some goals mean a great deal to us, some mean little or nothing, and all the others fall somewhere in between.

Many teachers are aware of the goals they have for their students; but frequently they are less clear as to the value they place on each goal. For the most part, this doesn't matter. An important goal is an important goal, and the degree of importance makes no real difference.

In conflict situations, however, your goals might be conflicting not only with those of a student, but also with other goals that you hold. For example, one of my goals is to teach children to be independent and to make choices about their activities. Another of my goals is to have children productively engaged about ninety percent of the time.

On the whole, these two goals are compatible. But in learning to be independent, children sometimes flounder (to put it mildly), and there are times when a child isn't productively engaged. I can simply assign work to such a student, and that will take care of the second goal. But it isn't really congruent with the first goal, building independence.

At this point, it helps to have an idea of how much I value a particular goal. If one of the goals is more highly valued, then I can pursue that goal with a clear intent and be more effective in my approach than if I were trying to achieve two conflicting goals simultaneously.

The value you place on a goal can vary with the student, the nature of the class as a whole, the time of year, the particular assignment, and even how you feel that day. For example, in September, work and study-habit goals rank high in my classroom because the students are learning what standard of work I expect from them. In March, such goals are less important because by then the students know what's expected (I hope), and an occasional lapse won't hurt them.

Exercise

The following exercise is a quick and easy way to rank the value of your goals.

1. Quickly list ten of your classroom goals. Don't worry about whether they're broad or specific. Any ten that come to mind will do.

2. Now rate each goal on the following scale:

1. extremely important goal—I'll never give it up

2. very important goal—I won't give it up easily

3. moderately important goal—I could go either way

4. unimportant goal—I don't really care about this one

5. worthless goal—I've been wasting my time

Ranking goals and values is most useful when you are defining particular student vs. teacher conflicts. As the teacher, it is your responsibility to define the problem clearly and to act rationally on that definition. Rather than seeing every student vs. teacher conflict as a threat to your power, approach it more logically.

Decide first of all if this is a conflict of goals. If so, what is your goal? How highly do you value it? Does the child have a conflicting goal? If so, state it if you can. Or is this a case of the child's not valuing your goal as highly as you do?

One advantage to this approach is that if you are clear about what goal is involved in the conflict and how important the goal is to you, then you are more likely to focus on that problem rather than to react defensively.

Needs

Of course, not all teacher-student conflicts are conflicts of goals. Frequently the needs of the teacher conflict with the needs of the child. When this happens, you are in the rather tricky position of having to be aware of your own needs and yet removed from them at the same time. As it usually happens, the more understanding you have of your own needs in a conflict situation, the better you will be able to step back from them and deal rationally with the conflict. This will better enable you to use your power constructively.

A quick way to categorize your needs as a teacher is to put them into one of four slots:

effectiveness—meeting goals, being competent at your job

self-esteem—feeling good about yourself

authority—being in control of yourself and your situation

positive interaction—being liked by others (including your students)

Awareness of needs helps you define the problem in a more useful way:

What needs do you have in this situation?

What needs does the child have?

How can both sets of needs be met?

How can you both win?

Finally, it is entirely possible for your goals to conflict with a student's needs, or vice versa, or for your needs *and* goals to conflict with those of the child. The thing to keep in mind is that it is often possible to meet everyone's needs and achieve everyone's goals. Everyone can win, and the cost of not at least trying is high indeed.

Putting It All Together— Effective Rule Making

It is possible to exercise your authority without being authoritarian. It is possible to reduce the number of petty and unimportant conflicts that arise from issues of power and to concentrate on the important ones. The first thing to do is to establish effective rules.

For years I started the school year by drawing up a list of rules with the help of my new class. The students told me what they thought I wanted to hear—no fighting, no running in the halls, no yelling in class, no spitting on people, that sort of thing. The list was posted somewhere in the room. And around mid-October, when everyone had forgotten all about it, the list would fall down and get put on a shelf somewhere, never to be seen again. The rules were enforced haphazardly and inconsistently, depending in part on my mood and in part on my sensitivity (or lack thereof) to the child and the situation that led to the rule's being broken.

This was not effective rule making. Effective Rules prescribe positive behavior and list of range of consequences for not behaving that way. Thus, a child knows exactly what behavior is expected, and what will happen if the rule is broken. The following exercise explains how to establish Effective Rules in a way that includes the class but also meets your need for control. It is presented as one exercise but will take several days in your classroom.

Exercise[1]

1. By yourself, think up all the rules you can. Write them down no matter how petty they may seem. Then go over the list and star those that seem most important to you, combining those that overlap and eliminating those that seem redundant or unimportant.

2. Now write down the ten to fifteen rules that seem most important to you. Write them in very specific terms. "Respect each other" is too vague. "Don't call people names" is specific. If at all possible, state them positively: "Call people what they want to be called" is better than "Don't call people names."

3. Present the rules to the class. *Explain the reason for each and every rule.* Now, are there any the students object to? Any they feel should be added? An alternative approach is to go through steps one and two with the class. (I have done it both ways, and there are advantages and disadvantages to both. Do what feels right for you.)

4. With the class, decide three or four consequences for breaking each rule. Consequences should relate to the rule and focus on the behavior involved. For example, if the rule says "Keep desk tops clean," the logical consequence for writing on a desk top should be cleaning the

desk top, as opposed to writing one hundred times "I will not write on desk tops." Describe the consequences very clearly so that students know exactly what will happen if they break a rule.

5. Prescribe a range of consequences from mild to strong. This way you can take into account extenuating circumstances. For example:

    Rule: People are not for hitting. Disputes should be settled peaceably through a conflict resolution technique.

    Consequences:

    1. Students get a warning.

    2. Students apologize to the teacher, to the class, and to each other.

    3. Students fill out a fight form (see chapter two).

    4. Students stay in from recess to practice conflict resolution techniques.

        Kids often want severe consequences for rule infractions. You must temper this extremism. In my class, nearly every rule has as a possible consequence a warning to stop, in addition to more severe consequences.

6. When the class agrees to the final list of rules and consequences, post a large master list in a prominent place. This may take up a lot of your bulletin board space, but it's worth it. Review the rules and consequences often, and even quiz the kids, until everyone, including yourself, knows them by heart.

7. You have to show the class that you mean business, that you expect them to follow the rules they agreed to, and that failure to do so will result in one of the consequences. Do not accept excuses or make exceptions. As I said earlier, the fact that you have available a range of possible consequences will allow you to take individual needs and extenuating circumstances into account.

You will probably find, as I did, that this sort of Effective Rule Making is worth the time it takes. Research indicates that conflicts increase when people are governed by a multitude of rules they had no part in developing. This procedure reduces conflicts and helps to prevent power abuses. It is also a valuable exercise in self-governing and decision making for the children.

Other Approaches to Rules

Not everyone is comfortable with the Effective Rule Making approach. Some find it too cumbersome; others, too structured. One teacher I know developed one set of consequences for all rules.

Whatever approach to rules and rule making you adopt, make sure that:

1. you can live with the rules

2. the children know what they are and understand the reason for each

3. you enforce them consistently

Punishment

If you adopt the Effective Rules approach, most of your punishments will be in the form of consequences. But there will always arise situations in which you as the teacher must exercise your authority and punish a child. Here are some suggestions for not abusing that authority.

1. Punish quickly and strongly enough to in fact punish, but don't be overly severe. Harsh punishment causes resentment and probably does not lastingly change behavior.

2. When you punish, be sure the student understands exactly why he or she is being punished and what behavior would have been more appropriate.

3. Never humiliate a child. Remember that the goal of punishment is to change behavior, not to exact revenge.

Exercise

Think of the times you have punished children recently, and why you chose to punish.

Imagine yourself as the child involved.

How would you feel if you were punished that way?

Would it help you to change your behavior?

Taking a moment to think "If this were applied to me, would it change my behavior?" can help you avoid harsh, humiliating, or abusive punishments. In fact, by and large, consequences work better than punishments.

Accentuating the Positive

I've found that it is easy to fall into the habit of dwelling on the negative with students and to neglect to praise them when they behave well. Looking for positive behavior and rewarding it pays off in several ways. It not only increases the likelihood of that behavior in the future, it also helps you feel better about the class and reminds you that things aren't as terrible as they may seem.

Approaching Student vs. Teacher Conflicts

Step 1: By the Rules

If you have adopted the Effective Rules approach and have established clear rules and consequences, most student vs. teacher conflicts in your room will relate somehow to these rules. In such a case, point out how the rule was broken and the effect that breaking it has on the class. (This reinforces the logical reasons for the rules.) State what the consequence will be. Accept no excuses. If you and the class have agreed to certain rules and consequences, then you must implement them consistently. If there are extenuating circumstances, and there frequently are, then you can take advantage of your range of options by imposing light consequences.

Step 2: One to One

If the child balks at the consequence or gives you a hard time, do not engage in a power struggle before the entire class. Instead, find a private place and confront him or her on a one-to-one basis. If appropriate, remind the student that he or she agreed to the rules and consequences. Find out why the child is resisting, and work out the details of the consequence with him or her.

Step 3: Conflict Resolution

If the student continues to resist, suggest a conflict resolution procedure. Step-by-step procedures have a calming effect because they are methodical. They allow you and the student to establish emotional distance from the problem and to focus on the problem rather than on yourselves.

Step 4: Third Party

If a conflict resolution technique fails to produce a satisfactory resolution, it may be time to call in a third party. This should be a teacher whom both you and the student trust. It is particularly important that the child not feel that the mediator is automatically on your side. The mediator can follow the mediation process outlined in chapter two or any of the conflict resolution techniques suggested in chapter two and this chapter. (On a couple of occasions, I have made use of student mediators, with excellent results.)

Step 5: Higher Authorities

If all else fails, your last resort is the principal or the child's parents or both. Depending on the child and his or her parents, you might want to enlist their aid right away, forgoing step four. As a rule, however, I'd suggest exhausting all other resources before appealing to higher authorities.

Always remember that, in addition to resolving a conflict, you are also serving as a model. Children will be watching you to see if your own conflict resolution technique is of a type that you insist they practice. Even if you are indeed very angry, it is particularly important not to lose control of yourself. If your temper is a problem, count to ten; and before doing anything else, ask youself:

Is what I'm about to do going to solve the problem?

Will it affirm the children involved?

Will it build trust and community?

Remember that even as you insist that children accept responsibility for the consequences of their actions, so must you.

Student vs. teacher conflicts are an opportunity to demonstrate that conflict is a source of growth. When any conflict is resolved, ask the children:

"What have we learned from this?"

"How will it make our classroom a better place to be?"

The following are conflict resolution techniques that are particularly useful in student vs. teacher conflicts. Several techniques from the previous chapter are also useful here, particularly reflective listening, role reversals, the problem puppets, and storytelling.

Again, I do not want to mislead you. No one can guarantee that following a step-by-step procedure will completely resolve a particular conflict. You must depend on your own common sense and your sensitivity to the child, to his or her needs, to your own needs, and to the situation. As always, if one approach fails, try another. Combine, adapt, and alter them. Above all, learn and grow from the experience.

I Statements

Grades K-6

Procedure:
An I statement is not a conflict resolution technique per se. Rather, it is a format for clearly stating your feelings about a situation in a way that doesn't accuse the other person. For this reason, you can use I statements with many conflict resolution techniques without making the other party defensive.

The following formats can be used for I statements:

"I feel [angry, frustrated, sad] when you —— because ——."

"I [resent it, dislike it, get frustrated] when you —— because ——."

"I [appreciate it, like it, enjoy it] when you ——."

"When you ——, I feel —— because ——."

Example:
Janet is wandering around the room, chatting with different people during reading group time, when she should be working at her desk. Ms. Adams says, "Janet, you seem to be out of your seat a lot."

J: I'm looking for a pencil.

Ms. A: Janet, when you wander around during reading time, I feel annoyed that you are not doing your work, and are disturbing others who are trying to work.

J: Okay. I found a pencil. I'll start working now.

Ms. A: Thank you.

Negotiating

Grades K-6

Procedure:
1. State the problem as you see it, in a way that does not assign blame but simply outlines the facts. Ask the child or children involved to confirm or to correct your summary.

2. State what you want and why. Have the child do the same.

3. Level with the student. State clearly what the limits are—what cannot be negotiated. Then say what can be negotiated and state several trade-offs you are willing to make. Have the child say what trade-offs he or she is willing to make. You may be more successful with young children if you have them describe some ways they would like to see the conflict resolved.

4. Work out an agreement that is mutually satisfactory.

Example:

Ronald is a third grader who has difficulty with math. One day Jim Hargrave, his teacher, notices him sitting at his desk, flipping through a library book when he should be working.

JH: Ronald, is your work finished?

R: [*sullen*] No.

JH: Get to it, please.

Ronald makes no response. A few minutes later, when Jim looks up from his reading group, he sees that Ronald is still leafing through the book. Jim gets up to speak to him.

JH: What's the problem? Why aren't you working?

R: I hate this. I'm not doing it anymore.

JH: Do you need help? I'll help you.

R: I don't want help. I hate this, that's all. I'm not doing it.

JH: You're tired of having to work so hard at math and don't see why you should continue, right?

R: Right. I'm not doing it anymore.

JH: I would like you to do the math. Do you remember when we talked about survival skills? [*Ronald nods.*] Well, being able to multiply was one of those skills. What would you like?

R: I told you. Not to do math ever again. It's boring.

JH: Well, Ronald, at some point today, you have to do the work; you know that. We have gym this afternoon; and if you want to go, the math must be finished. But you don't have to do it this minute. Is your reading work done yet? [*Ronald shakes his head.*] You could do reading, then math. Or do one row of problems, then reading, then another row of problems, then spelling, then the rest of the math problems. What do you think?

R: Will you stay here and help me?

JH: I can't stay here now, but we could do it during recess.

R: I don't want to miss recess.

JH: How about lunch? We could eat lunch in here, and do a problem, then have a bite, do another problem, and have another bite. Like that.

R: [*laughing*] That's funny. Let's do that.

This situation involved a young child, and so the teacher had to supply the alternatives. Ronald is obviously a child who requires some babying, and Jim is clearly willing to baby him, even if it means working through lunch time. That was a choice Jim had to make, based on his sensitivity to Ronald's needs.

Notice that Jim made the limits very clear—the math would be finished by afternoon or no gym.

When you negotiate with a child, you must also know your own limits. If you are one of those people who has trouble with the very idea of negotiating with a student, then accept that fact, and avoid negotiating. (But you might find it useful to think about why you feel this way.) Whatever you do, don't begin to negotiate and then back out when the dialogue goes in a direction you don't like, or proceeds too slowly for your taste. Students perceive such behavior as simply a capricious use of power.

Behavior Contracts

Grades K–6

Materials: pencil, paper

Procedure:

Sometimes a child refuses to follow a particular rule or accept a consequence, or is always breaking many rules and is a continual disturbance in the classroom. In such a case, you may want to negotiate a behavior contract. I'm not recommending that you set up new rules for this particular student. Instead, work with the student toward finding a way for him or her to follow the classroom rules.

1. Meet with the student one to one. Explain the problem as you see it and clearly state the limits. Have the student explain his or her action and why he or she cannot seem to follow the rules.

2. Acknowledge his or her feelings. Ask what the student needs in order to obey the rule.

3. Try to work out a compromise between what the student has said and the limits you've established. Use such techniques as I statements and reflective listening to facilitate the process.

4. When an agreement has been reached, write up a contract stating clearly what the student will do and what you will do. Both parties sign the agreement.

5. If no agreement can be reached, suggest a postponement until the next school day, or ask the child to suggest someone as a mediator.

6. If the contract doesn't work, renegotiate it. If after three or more tries it still doesn't work, enlist the aid of higher authorities.

Example:

Barbara Fisher's first grade class had a clear rule about name-calling. Every day, Marie broke this rule. Barbara had imposed all the prescribed consequences many times. Now she has decided to negotiate a behavioral contract with Marie.

BF: Marie, we have a rule about name-calling that you have broken often this past week. You've suffered the consequences each time, but you haven't stopped. Can you tell me why?

M: I don't like those girls over there.

BF: Why?

M: They won't let me play. Fat brats!

BF: Does calling them names make them want to play with you?

M: No.

BF: What could we do to help you not call people names?

M: They make me mad.

BF: You get mad and call them names, right? [*Marie nods.*] It would make me mad, too, if they wouldn't let me play. But calling them names doesn't help. How about this—if you'll agree not to call them names for three days, I'll arrange for you to work with Jean and Susan on a project. Then they'll see how nice you really are.

M: Make them be nice to me.

BF: Well, I can talk to them about giving you a chance. Then, if they try hard and you try hard, you won't have to call them names, okay?

M: Okay.

Contract :

Marie agrees to make a model town with Jean and Susan. She will work with them for three days without calling them names, no matter how angry she gets. Ms. Fisher agrees to talk to Jean and Susan about giving Marie a chance.

Signed : _____

_____

Classroom rules are important, but so are children. In this student vs. student vs. teacher conflict, Barbara listened carefully to Marie, affirmed her and the validity of her anger, and gently insisted that she follow the rule.

In instances such as this, teachers are often concerned about letting students get away with something, or about setting a bad precedent. These are valid concerns, but let me reemphasize that, despite the compromises you may have to make, your goal is to help the student obey the rule. Don't enter negotiations willing to hand the student everything; then he or she really will be getting away with something. However, neither should you expect the student to do all the compromising. As for setting a bad precedent, i.e., rewarding disruptive behavior with special contracts and attention, let me say that disruptive behavior is always rewarded with special attention, usually in the form of class time wasted. This approach is far more productive.

Worksheet in Upgrading Behavior[2]

Grades 3–6

Procedure:

This is a technique that helps students focus on specific forms of behavior they would like to change. It is not a conflict resolution technique as such, but it can reduce conflict. It is particularly appropriate for students who get into frequent conflicts because of certain ways of acting, and who are interested in changing their ways.

1. Discuss with the student what particular behavior seems to get him or her into trouble most often. Once this behavior is identified, ask if the student is interested in changing.

2. If the answer is yes, show the worksheet in upgrading behavior (see Appendix), and explain that filling it out is a way of focusing on a form of behavior in order to change it.

3. Help the student fill out the worksheet, discussing frankly the different parts of it. Filling out the worksheet requires the student to describe the behavior pattern that needs to be changed and the circumstances that seem to evoke the behavior. The form asks what the pattern gains the student (the payoff) and keeps the student from getting (the cost). Then the student decides whether the payoff outweighs the cost or vice versa, and whether or not a change is therefore in order. Finally, the student describes a new form of behavior that he or she could try the next time the triggering situation arises. Don't mislead the student into thinking that changing behavior is easy, but do emphasize the benefits of doing so. Assure the student of your availability for support.

4. You might try role-playing some situations with the student to give him or her a chance to practice new behavior.

Example:

Martin was a sixth grader who usually left his homework undone. Overweight and neglected by his parents, Martin's poor self-concept and sense of failure were evident to his teacher, Paul Rousseau. Paul has approached Martin with the idea of the worksheet in upgrading behavior and stressed the advantages of changing his pattern, particularly now, in the sixth grade, before he reaches junior high. Paul went through the worksheet with Martin and discussed the various aspects of it.

The approach worked, but Paul had to provide much support. Once the behavior had clearly changed, however, Martin approached Paul about using the worksheet to improve other ways of acting.

In Martin's case, a poor self-concept and its repercussions couldn't be cleared up overnight. In such situations, the advantage of the worksheet in upgrading behavior is that it provides a clear, systematic way of examining and improving one behavior pattern at a time. Although its use is limited by its contingency on the student's genuine desire to change, its success can be dramatic and heartening.

Behavior Modification

Grades K–6

Procedure:

All conflict resolution is an attempt to modify behavior. The procedure described below is a systematic approach to changing children's action so that it is more congruent with the goals, standards, or procedures of the classroom community. (For some people, this procedure raises ethical questions concerning manipulation. Although you must address these for yourself, I have tried to answer some of them by being very honest with my students about what I am trying to accomplish and why.)

1. Identify the behavior to be changed. Be as specific as you can with respect to what behavior you will try to extinguish and what you will reward.

2. Decide what the reward will be and how the reward system will work. For example, you might record positive behavior via a record card, a graph, or tokens. When a certain number of stars, tokens, or whatever has been accumulated, then the child (or children) earn a reward.

3. Present your behavior modification plan to the student or students involved (it may be the entire class). Explain what behavior you are trying to modify *and why*. Ask if it is agreed that change is warranted. Explain the reward system thoroughly, emphasizing that you are rewarding the positive behavior that occurs.

4. Once the student or students understand and agree to the procedure, implement it.

Example:

Tom Chang had a messy third grade. He could not trace the problem to individuals; rather, the problem lay with the entire class—they constantly littered the classroom, left the sink messy, kept the books and games in disarray, and generally took no pride in the classroom's appearance. Tom pointed this out to the class many times, and the class had made a rule with consequences concerning mess, but to no avail.

Tom decided to try behavior modification. He purchased a large, attractive puzzle he knew the class would enjoy. He made a job chart assigning everyone some sort of clean-up task, and made another chart with a plus side and a minus side, to record progress.

He explained the procedure. To earn the puzzle, the class had to keep the room immaculate for a week. Each student was responsible for his or her job, and there would be several spot checks every day. If the room was clean, the class earned a plus on the progress chart. If it wasn't clean, a minus was recorded. More pluses than minuses at the end of the week earned the class the puzzle.

This was a very effective way of clearing up a certain kind of behavior that led to a student vs. teacher conflict. Since it eliminated an unimportant conflict, Tom had no reservations about using it.

The term *behavior modification* brings to mind rat mazes and M&M's. The procedure need not be crass, however, nor, I might add, when it is done in the way that I've outlined, is it really possible to manipulate the children without their consent. There are, of course, times and situations to which this technique is inappropriate; but it can be a simple, positive, and effective way to eliminate unnecessary and petty conflicts.

Problem-Solving Techniques

Grades K–6

Procedure:

A problem-solving technique is a fun and effective way to resolve some types of conflicts. Assess the conflict first. Some types, particularly value conflicts, are not amenable to solution by this technique.

People are always developing multistepped problem-solving techniques. (I came across one recently that gave teachers seventeen steps to follow.) Basically, they all boil down to this:

1. *Define the problem.* Phrase the definition so that it focuses on the problem, not on the people involved. And, as I discussed in chapter one, try not to promote solutions in your definition.

2. *Produce solutions.* Think of as many ways to solve the problem as you can. (Suggestions for teaching students how to brainstorm are in chapter four.)

3. *Choose and act.* Choose a solution, or combine a couple of them; then act. This step is crucial, obviously, because ideas for wonderful solutions do no good if no action is taken.

Example:

The second grade desks are arranged in straight rows. Whenever the teacher, Jane McLaughlin, has tried to arrange the desks in clusters or lines, so much talking results that it's soon back to rows. The children have been asking her for another chance. Jane decided to use the problem-solving method.

First she explained its procedure to the class. Then she defined the problem: "You'd like to sit in groups because it's cozier, and you can be near your friends and make new ones. Whenever we've tried it in the past, there has been too much talking. Would you agree?" The children nodded. "When you talk so much, I have a hard time working with you individually and in reading groups. Also, that much noise makes me nervous and grouchy. Now I'd like to see if we can come up with a way to keep the noise down when the desks are in groups. Raise your hand if you have an idea. Don't worry if it sounds silly—I want to write everything down."

Here are some of the ideas the class came up with:

1. Punish kids who talk.

2. Make it a rule that everyone has to whisper.

3. Everyone has to pass notes.

4. Only people who don't talk get to sit in groups.

5. Put cardboard walls between the desks.

6. Give kids who talk a ticket, like a speeding ticket, for talking.

7. If kids get five tickets, they miss gym.

8. People who talk get kissed on the lips.

9. Kids who talk stand in the corner for five minutes.

When the students could come up with no more ideas, Jane and the class discussed them one by one, erasing those they felt had no real promise. Ultimately, they expanded on one: the group got tickets even if only one child talked. After three tickets, the group lost a privilege for that day. Jane agreed to remind the class each day of their promise to work quietly.

It was perhaps unfortunate that a more positive solution could not be reached in this situation, but because the children helped to develop the solution, they also had a real stake in implementing it.

It's important that children understand the procedure thoroughly, and it helps if they've had experience brainstorming (see chapter four). If you begin a problem-solving session, you should not back out. If the adopted idea ultimately fails, try another problem-solving session.

Classroom Meetings[3]

Grades K–6

Procedure:

There are many uses for classroom meetings: discussions, sharing feelings, solving problems, classroom business, even show and tell. They can also be effective forums for conflict resolution.

1. Before you use them for conflict resolution, get your class accustomed to classroom meetings. First and foremost, a child must feel safe participating. Rules regarding conduct in a meeting should be developed and strictly enforced. Children of all ages can learn to take turns, listen respectfully, and not laugh at other people's contributions. (Chapter five has suggestions for improving discussion skills.)

2. In classroom meetings, you should participate as well as moderate. Share yourself as you expect the children to do.

3. Once your class is at ease with the classroom meeting format—which shouldn't take too long—there are two ways to use it for conflict resolution. One is to have a "Why do we do this?" discussion. Here you can talk about the reasons for classroom procedure and curriculum. (One reason student vs. teacher conflicts develop is that no one bothers to explain to children why they are required to do the things they are required to do.) The second type of discussion is the "What can we do about this?" kind, in which you talk about a problem that currently exists.

4. In both types of meeting, everyone who wants to participate should get a fair chance to share his or her feelings and opinions. Encourage the students to listen reflectively and to focus on the problem, not the personalities involved.

5. Try to keep the meeting lively; don't let it drag. Try to end on a positive note, either by reflecting on the good results of the meeting or by agreeing with the class to take positive action.

Example:

Lesly Johnson's sixth grade acts sophisticated and blasé. The class as a whole can work up no enthusiasm for anything, and those students who do get excited about a subject quickly have their excitement dampened by the group's negativity.

Having called a classroom meeting, Lesly explains how she feels.

LJ: I work hard to develop lessons and to find materials that will interest you, but it doesn't seem to work. This class is no fun for you and no fun for me. I would like to get to the bottom of this. Let's go around the circle and have everyone complete this sentence: "School would be wonderful if ———."

This is relatively successful. There *are* things the class is interested in. However, the three Rs are not among them.

LJ: I notice that traditional subjects weren't mentioned too often. But we can't just study sports and race cars and that sort of thing.

1:   Mrs. Johnson, we're almost in junior high. Can't we study things like they do?

2:   We're too old for the reading books. I like to read. Can't I read books I like from the media center?

LJ: But how would we keep track of your progress? How would I grade you? [*Class groans.*] I know that you don't care about that sort of thing, but your parents do.

3:   Give us tests and stuff. We could keep records in a folder or something.

2:   Could we do more projects? The other sixth grades do projects a lot.

4:   Yeah, projects! That would be great.

LJ: Let me ask you something. Is it the material we study that makes you so negative, or the way we study it? [*Class is confused.*] Let me rephrase that. First, do you think you have a negative attitude? [*Class nods.*] Why?

5: I don't know. It's kind of boring the way we do things.

3: Yeah, the same way we've always done them.

1: In junior high, they don't do things the way we do.

6: Shut up about junior high!

LJ: Let me propose this. We'll continue with our regular curriculum for the next two weeks. In that time, I'll work with a small group exploring more creative ways to learn the subject matter we have to learn. Are there people who would like to work with me? [*Hands go up.*] All right, I'll meet with you later. Now, about that attitude: can you start working on a more positive attitude? [*Affirmations from the class.*] That will be your part of the bargain.

Lesly took some real risks here—probably more than she realized at first—by putting herself and her curriculum before the class for criticism. She stayed in control of the process, redefining the problem as necessary, and calmly negotiated an equitable arrangement with her class.

Notice that she respected the children's criticisms as valid but made clear that her dissatisfaction with their negative attitude also was valid. She was perceptive enough to know that you can't force people to be positive and that openness and willingness to change on her part were therefore essential.

Notes

1. Many teachers contributed ideas to the Effective Rule Making procedure. I would particularly like to thank Sheila Edlestein.
2. Gerald Weinstein and Mario D. Fantini, *Toward Humanistic Education* (New York: Praeger, 1972). Used with permission of the copyright holder, the Ford Foundation.
3. For a detailed discussion of classroom meetings, see William Glasser, *Schools Without Failure* (New York: Harper and Row, 1969), chap. 10.

Chapter 4

Teaching Students to Be Peacemakers

Preventing conflicts is the work of politics;
establishing peace is the work of education.
—*Maria Montessori*

When I first started teaching, I encouraged and even insisted that the children bring all their conflicts to me. It seemed the only alternative to letting them slug it out in a corner. Within a few days I learned that I had made a terrible mistake. Everywhere I went I was followed by a line of kids, and each one had some complaint or another. I felt more like a referee than a teacher.

With or without encouragement, students often bring their conflicts to the teacher for resolution. Left on their own, they are usually trapped in the aggression-passivity dilemma. Appealing to adult authority seems to be the only way out. It need not be, however; and one of the goals of creative conflict resolution is to help children learn how to resolve their own conflicts, nonviolently.

Since that is a somewhat ambitious goal, let's look at it more closely. What does it mean to teach students to be peacemakers? Essentially, it means trying to show them that there are realistic and workable alternatives to aggression and passivity. This requires that children understand the nature of conflict, that they learn the skills necessary for approaching conflict in new ways, and that they be trained in conflict resolution techniques.

Conflict resolution experts have identified many skills that facilitate the smooth management of conflict. Some of these will be treated in succeeding chapters: cooperation and communication skills, the ability to express feelings constructively, and tolerance of diversity. The four we will be discussing here are what I call the basic skills of conflict resolution. They are:

1. analysis—defining the conflict
2. ideation—developing alternative solutions
3. strategy—gaining a working knowledge of conflict resolution techniques
4. risk-taking—choosing to act on solutions[1]

During actual conflict resolution, these skills are not discrete. The lessons that follow focus on the skills separately only to introduce them and to heighten children's awareness of them. When choosing activities, be guided by your knowledge of your students, their needs, their interests, and the approaches that generally work best for them.

I strongly recommend that you make the lessons as relevant as possible to the children. Give them experiences from which they can learn and help them to apply this learning to their daily lives. Once you've introduced the skills and concepts, don't let them die. Give the kids opportunities to practice the skills and to integrate them into actual conflict resolution. Suggestions for structured practice and for taking advantage of teachable moments are included later in this chapter.

Don't forget, an important way to make the lessons stick is to model the behavior you want. When children see you defining problems, coming up with some alternatives, and acting as if conflicts had win-win solutions, they are powerfully affected.

It's important to remember that creative conflict resolution is not aimed at turning children into pacifists. You may make a rule against violence in your classroom or on the playground, but when you discuss conflict with your students, you should always acknowledge that it is an option. Kids know this already simply by looking around them. We are saying, simply, that there are usually other, more effective ways to resolve conflicts.

This chapter contains descriptions of activities grouped under the following headings:

What Is Conflict?

Analysis Skills

Ideation Skills

Strategy Skills

Acting

Practice

What Is Conflict?

An examination of the nature of conflict seems a pretty unlikely topic for elementary school. As a matter of fact, it's a topic that interests children greatly. Conflict is something that has a real impact on their lives.

This section contains activities to help you explore the following questions with your students:

What is conflict?

How does it affect me?

How do I respond to it?

Also in this section are suggestions for introducing the concept of win-win conflict resolution. Since many of the lessons in this book refer to this concept, please be sure children are exposed to it and understand it.

Conflict Web

Grades 3–6

Materials: chalkboard and chalk, or a very large sheet of paper with crayons or markers

Procedure:

This activity gives students learning about conflict a look at the big picture.

1. In the center of the paper, write the word "Conflict" and circle it.

2. Ask the class what the word means and what associations and memories it evokes. Each time something is suggested, draw a solid line from the main circle and add the word or phrase:

3. As students begin suggesting ideas related to those previously suggested, link them not to the main circle but to the appropriate previous contribution.

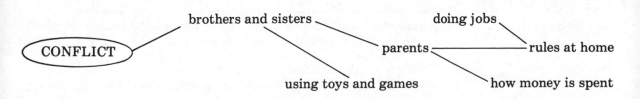

Continue the web as long as interest remains high.

Discussion:

How could we define conflict?

What elements do all conflicts seem to have in common?

What causes conflict?

What makes it worse?

What cools it off?

What Is Conflict?

Grades (K, 1), 2–6

Materials: dictionaries, or pictures showing conflicts

Procedure:

1. Have students look up and share several definitions of conflict. Note the details of these definitions on the board, and help the class develop a single definition.

2. Ask for examples of conflicts—give a few if necessary. Ask about conflicts

> between friends
>
> in families
>
> in oneself
>
> between countries
>
> between students and teachers

3. Have the class come up with a list of conflict-related terms, and distinguish among them: What is a fight? An argument? Are all conflicts fights?

Discussion:

What kinds of things cause conflicts?

What makes a conflict worse?

What makes a conflict better?

With younger children, use the conflict pictures instead of dictionary definitions as a starting point for discussion.

Types of Conflict

Grades 2–6

Materials: three-by-five-inch index cards, sort charts (pieces of paper, each with three sections labeled *resources, needs,* and *values*)

Procedure:

1. Write the terms *resources, needs,* and *values* on the board. Discuss their meanings with the class.

2. Distribute five three-by-five cards to each student and have him or her describe five different conflicts. They need not have actually occurred, nor do the descriptions need to be elaborate.

3. Have the students work in groups of three or four. Give each group a sort chart. Have the students read their descriptions to their own groups. Each group should then try to categorize the conflicts described.

4. Any vague or hard-to-classify conflicts can be set aside for a whole-class discussion of where they belong.

Discussion:

What were some [resource, need, value] conflicts?

How did you decide where they went on the chart?

What were some of the factors you looked at?

How do these categories relate to the causes of conflict?

What were some of the conflicts that you couldn't classify easily?

More Conflict Categories

Grades 3–6

Procedure:

Conflict categories make interpretation and resolution of conflicts easier. Although conflict resolution experts favor needs, resources, values, and sometimes goals as categories, students may not find these meaningful. Help them develop other categorization schemes, such as:

simple-confusing

friendly-angry

silly-important

violent-nonviolent

resolvable-unresolvable

Discussion:

What are some other ways you might classify conflicts?

What criteria might you use?

How might these classifications help you resolve conflicts?

Positive Effects of Conflict

Grades K–3

Materials: pictures of family conflicts or pictures of things over which families might conflict (e.g., new TV, vacation places)

Procedure:

1. Discuss the nature of the conflict in a particular picture. Have the students relate it to their own lives.

2. Have children write, draw, or discuss a positive resolution to the conflict defined. Share the responses, and note the similarities and the variety.

Discussion:

Have you ever had a similar conflict in your family? How did you handle it?

How are these responses similar? Different?

Should everyone in the family be happy with the solution?

If you were in the family, would you be happy with the solution?

What would some positive effects of this conflict be?

What might be some effects of not dealing with the conflict at all?

Useful Conflicts

Grades 4–6

Materials: pencils, paper

Procedure:

1. Have students be on the lookout over the course of a week for a conflict that is resolved functionally (in a way that serves a useful purpose).

2. At the end of the week, have them write about the conflict, describing it and its resolution. Also have them explain why it served a useful purpose and why the resolution was functional, not dysfunctional.

3. Students who couldn't find a functional conflict can describe a dysfunctional one and tell how it might have been resolved functionally.

🍎 I ask my students to stay on the lookout for conflicts handled functionally and to tell the whole class about them.

Discussion:

What did the people involved learn from the conflict you told about?

What did you learn from it?

What things help a conflict to be resolved functionally?

Was it difficult finding a functional conflict?

Wasting Time

Grades K–6

Procedure:

1. Have the class develop a list of unnecessary conflicts that waste time in your classroom.

2. Discuss one of the conflicts, how it develops, and what could be changed either to avoid it or to prevent violence (if violence attends it).

Discussion:

How is this conflict a waste of time?

Why is it persistent in our classroom?

What do we need to change to eliminate it?

What might be some of the consequences of those changes?

Animal Weapons

Grades K-6

Materials: pictures of animals with bared teeth, claws, quills, antlers, horns, or actual antlers, horns, teeth, etc.

Procedure:
Show the pictures or objects and ask the questions listed below to initiate discussion on how animals defend themselves. When comparing people with animals, emphasize that our minds set us apart, enabling us both to create horrible weapons and to avoid weapons altogether.

Discussion:

How do animals use parts of their bodies to defend themselves?

In what situations will animals do that?

How is that similar to what people will do? Dissimilar?

What is it that enables us not to use weapons?

What are our alternatives to weapons?

Is Everybody Happy?

Grades K-2

Procedure:

1. Describe a conflict to the class. For instance, you could say that Irene is putting a puzzle together in an open space on the floor. The puzzle has lots of pieces and would be very difficult to move. Patty has a large sheet of paper to make a mural. The only place she can find that is large enough for the paper is the place where Irene is working. Patty has asked Irene to move, but Irene says no.

2. Ask, "Is Irene happy? Is Patty? How could they solve their problem?"

3. Solicit several possible resolutions. Ask, of each one, "Would that make everybody happy?" Explain that an "Is everybody happy?" resolution is called a win-win solution, because both (or all) the people win.

4. Repeat with other conflict situations.

Discussion:

What would make everybody happy in this situation?

Why would that be nice?

Why would that be better than a situation where someone wins and someone loses?

Winning and Losing

Grades 1-6

Procedure:

1. Describe to the class the following situation. Angie wants to play with the class gerbils. Denise wants to put them into a maze she has built for a science experiment. Ask, "What's the problem here? What does Angie want? What does Denise want? Why?" Have the class

discuss briefly who should get what; then ask for a vote. Tabulate the results and note that either Angie wins or Denise wins and that's that.

2. Say that there are other ways to look at resolving conflicts. Place the following chart on the board:

	Angie gets what she wants	Angie doesn't get what she wants
Denise gets what she wants	win-win	win-lose
Denise doesn't get what she wants	win-lose	lose-lose

Ask, "What would be an example of a win-win resolution? Win-lose? Lose-lose? What about Angie and Denise? What would be a win-win resolution for them? Could you have a positive lose-lose situation?" (Yes, you can—a compromise is technically a lose-lose resolution.)

Inner Conflicts

Grades 1–6

Procedure:

1. Ask volunteers to describe choices they have made this week. These need not be complicated—choosing a strawberry vs. chocolate ice cream cone or going to a movie vs. watching TV will do.

2. On the chalkboard, draw a large outline of a head with a line down the middle. On each side of the line, write an option in each decision:

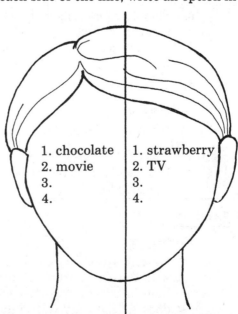

3. Explain that an inner conflict is a conflict within a person between needs, values, or desires for resources.

4. Try to get older students to describe their inner conflicts over needs and values (they will tend to talk about conflicts between desires for resources). Have students make their own diagrams and include in them an example of each type of conflict.

Discussion:

How can you or do you resolve inner conflicts?

How do your inner conflicts affect others?

What role does your conscience play in inner conflicts?

Violence—Good and Bad

Grades (K, 1), 2–6   **Procedure:**

1. Describe to the students a violent conflict that could arise among children at their grade level.

2. Discuss what could be called the positive aspects of violence in this situation—in other words, how violence is getting people what they want. List these payoffs on the board. Then discuss the negative aspects of violence. List these on the board. The negative will outweigh the positive.

🍎 With young children, this discussion works well with the problem puppets (see chapter two).

Discussion:

Did violence lead to a win-win resolution?

Did it get people what they really wanted?

What might have been a better resolution?

What are some things you might fight about?

What might be better resolutions to those conflicts?

Why do we have a rule against fighting in school?

TV Violence

Grades 3–6   **Procedure:**

Much can and should be done to teach students to be critical viewers of television. Here are two suggestions.

1. Have students keep a log for one night or one week, recording what TV shows they watch and how many acts of violence they see. Decide beforehand with the class how violence will be categorized: fistfights, murders, brawls, etc.

2. Have students poll family, friends, and neighbors concerning their attitudes toward TV violence. Questions for the poll can be developed in class.

Discussion:

What did you learn about TV violence?

Were you aware of the amount of violence you were exposed to?

How will your new awareness affect the way you watch TV?

Conflict Vocabulary Chart

Grades 2–6

Materials: chart paper, marking pen or crayon

Procedure:

1. Make a conflict vocabulary chart. Each time you add a word to the chart, write it on the board also, and have the class read it and try to explain what it means. Then discuss the meaning as it relates to conflict, and elicit examples from the children's lives.

2. Give certain terms special treatment, explaining their subtleties or relating them to creative conflict resolution.

   apologize (admit)—To say something like "I'm sorry; I was wrong."

   apologize (explain)—To say something like "I'm sorry this happened" when giving an explanation that clears up a misunderstanding. One need not have been in the wrong to apologize in this sense.

   compromise—A resolution in which each person gives up something to reach a satisfying agreement. Point out to the kids that, although compromise is often necessary, it is in fact a lose-lose resolution.

   escalate, de-escalate—Kids love these words. Make up a list of things that might cause a conflict to escalate or de-escalate.

   mediate, negotiate—See Negotiating and Mediating (activities described in the Strategy section later in this chapter).

   resources, needs, values—Relate these terms to the causes of conflict.

   aggression—Behavior aimed at harming another.

Conflict Vocabulary Activities

Grades 2–6

Procedure:

1. On ditto masters, make a crossword puzzle, a word search puzzle, or a scrambled word puzzle of the conflict vocabulary your class has mastered.

2. You can also make up conflict vocabulary worksheets on which students fill in blanks or match words with definitions.

3. Use the conflict vocabulary as a basis for dictionary work, spelling practice, writing assignments, and alphabetizing.

Some conflict-related terms are:

conflict	affirmation	aggressive	prejudice
conflict	cooperation	assertive	tolerance
resolution	compromise	anger	intolerance
mediate	escalate	hostility	fight
negotiate	de-escalate	frustration	argument
reconciliation	resources	violence	disagreement
peace	needs	nonviolence	apologize
war	values	pacifist	behavior
trust			

Symbols

Grades 1–6

Materials: pictures of symbols, drawing paper, crayons

Procedure:

1. Discuss symbols, beginning with mathematical symbols and progressing to such symbols as traffic signs and international symbols. Have students develop symbolic representations of conflict vocabulary.

2. Sign language is also symbolic. Students enjoy learning the signed equivalents of conflict vocabulary.

Discussion:

Why are symbols useful?

Are the symbols you invented concrete or abstract?

Which words were easiest to symbolize?

Analysis Skills

As I discussed in chapter one, the way a conflict is defined is crucial to establishing the search for a win-win solution; the definition must take into account the needs of the participants. But I have also found the problem definition technique described in chapter one is too sophisticated for most elementary children to master. You can, however, successfully help them to observe carefully what is going on and then state who is involved, what they want, and what the problem is. These three factors are enough to define the problem adequately, particularly if the children understand that they are searching for a win-win solution.

In the activities described below, remind children that they want to promote win-win rather than win-lose resolutions as they formulate definitions of problems.

Causes of Conflict

Grades 3–6

Materials: three-by-five-inch index cards, tape

Procedure:

1. Distribute two or three three-by-five cards to each student. On each card, have them describe a situation that might cause a conflict.

2. On the board, write "Lack of Cooperation," "Poor Communication," "Intolerance," and "Poor Conflict Resolution." Leave space under each term. Discuss the meaning of each and how it relates to conflict.

3. Have each student first read his or her cards aloud and then go to the board and tape the cards under the appropriate headings. Or read the cards yourself and discuss with the class where they belong.

4. Causes that don't fit the categories can be grouped under "Miscellaneous."

Discussion:

Why is it useful to know the causes of conflict?

What seems to be the most common cause?

What does this mean to all of us in relation to our behavior here?

Powerful People

Grades 3–6

Materials: pencils, paper

Procedure:

Have each student list five to ten of the most powerful people in his or her life and write a sentence saying why each person is powerful. Have student volunteers talk about some of the people they have listed. Use what they say as a basis for a discussion of the power dynamic in conflicts.

Discussion:

Do these people think they are powerful?

How do you know they are powerful?

How do they use their power?

What do they have in common?

How are they different?

What kinds of conflict do you have with powerful people?

How can you handle conflict with people who have more power than you?

Analysis Checklist

Grades K–6

Procedure:

1. Ask the class, "If you were a mediator or problem solver and you were going to help some of the kids in this class resolve a conflict, what would you need to know before you could resolve it?"

2. List all the suggestions on the board. When there are no more suggestions being made, discuss which ones are similar and which don't seem really useful. Combine similar ones and erase useless ones until you have a list of five or so.

3. Arrange the list in order of importance. Label the final list *Conflict Analysis Checklist*. Explain that this list shows the kind of information you need to resolve a conflict in a win-win manner.

4. Your checklist might look something like this, although only fourth through sixth graders are likely to come up with the last two items:

   1. Who's involved?
   2. What did they do?
   3. How did they do it?
   4. What does A want? What does B want? Etc.
   5. What type of conflict is it?
   6. What are the needs of the parties?

Discussion:

How would this information be helpful?

What would you do with the information once you had it?

Why might it be helpful to be able to analyze a conflict in this way?

Eyewitnesses

Grades K–3

Materials: microphone (real or pretend), conflict picture

Procedure:

1. Have the children examine the picture for thirty seconds.
2. With the microphone, ask a child to tell "our TV audience" what was happening in the picture. Interview several children.

Discussion:

Did all the analysis checklist questions get answered?

Did it matter?

What were the differences in different people's accounts?

Conflict Scripts

Grades 4–6

Materials: conflict pictures or newspaper accounts of conflicts

Procedure:

1. Give each student or pair of students either a conflict picture or a newspaper account of a conflict. Have them write scripts for the conflicts that will reveal the information required by the conflict analysis checklist.
2. Have students act out the scripts and, with the class, develop definitions of each conflict. Use the questions below as guides.

Discussion:

What information do we have?

What information don't we have?

How could we find out more?

Do we need to develop a good definition?

🍎 As a variation, save the scripts for performance as skits in which alternative solutions are developed.

Conflict Time Line

Grades 2–4

Procedure:

1. If students do not already know what time lines are, explain. Describe a sample conflict, and chart its development on a time line on the board.

2. Brainstorm possible solutions and have the children choose one they like. Include the solution on the time line, along with a possible consequence of the resolution.

3. Have students chart on time lines conflicts they have experienced.

Discussion:

What does the time line show about how conflicts [develop, escalate, de-escalate]?

Over how long a period did your conflict take place?

At what point on the time line could you intervene to de-escalate or resolve the conflict?

How would you do that?

The Other Side

Grades 2–4, (5, 6)

Materials: two pair of paper footprints, point-of-view cards (see below)

Procedure:

1. In advance, make point-of-view cards by writing on three-by-five-inch index cards descriptions of situations such as the following.

John feels he has too much homework and decides not to do any more science homework. How might his teacher feel?

Angel sees Kathy's good sweater on the floor of the gym and picks it up to return. As Angel carries it down the hall, she decides to try it on. Kathy sees her doing this. How might Kathy feel?

Phil has finished all his reading work in a hurry so that he can play with the trucks. Denise is already playing with the trucks. How does Denise feel?

2. Attach the footprints to the floor so that they are facing each other.

3. Explain to the class that it helps resolve conflicts if you understand the other person's point of view or stand in his or her footsteps. Have a student stand on one pair of footprints and draw a card from the deck of point-of-view cards. He or she should read the card aloud,

stand on the other pair of footprints, and state the other point of view.

Discussion:

Was it easy or hard to say what the other person felt?

Did you agree with one person more than the other?

Why would understanding the other point of view help to resolve conflicts?

🍎 Older students may balk at the footprint part, but then again, they may not. You know your class best.

Historical Conflicts

Grades 4–6

Procedure:

1. Have students work in groups. Either assign historical periods and places to each group (for instance, colonial America, pre-Columbian America, medieval Europe, ancient Greece, etc.), or tie this activity to a historical period the class is already studying.

2. Have each group research daily life in that period and report on the conflicts that young people faced and how they might have resolved them. Encourage students to imagine the possible consequences of each resolution they suggest.

Discussion:

How did you locate the information you needed?

Did biographies of famous people reveal conflicts?

How were conflicts in this period similar to yours? Different?

Ideation Skills

Developing new ideas is the crux of creative conflict resolution. It is also the most challenging and rewarding aspect. There's nothing quite like the feeling that comes with getting a new idea that works.

Getting new ideas is easier said than done. As I noted in chapter one, we tend to get so used to two or three ways of responding to conflict that getting a fresh perspective is difficult. Keep reminding yourself when a conflict seems unresolvable that somewhere there is a solution.

Actually, children tend to be very good at ideation. Being younger, they are more flexible in their thinking—less likely to reject unusual ideas, less likely to get stuck. The following activities give students practice in creating alternatives and provide suggestions for helping them understand the process of ideation.

Creativity should, of course, be encouraged throughout the school curriculum. The Bibliography of Resources lists several books that can help you promote it.

Introducing Brainstorming

Grades K–6

Materials: unusual material with which the class can make something (a very large cardboard box, a long cardboard tube, a large piece of fabric, an old piece of furniture)

Procedure:

1. Explain that the goal of brainstorming is to develop as many ideas as possible, as quickly as possible. The rules are:

    1. Defer judgment. Record all ideas, as quickly as possible.

    2. Build on previous ideas. Don't wait for completely original ideas; but combine, modify, and extend those already suggested.

    3. Don't hold back, but write down everything. Push for quantity.

2. Place the material you have brought in front of the children. Say that you want to use this to decorate the room but aren't sure what to do with it. Suggest that the class try brainstorming ideas.

3. Write on the chalkboard all the ideas the children suggest. Add a few of your own if necessary. Keep the pace very quick, and remind the children not to censor their ideas.

4. When no one has any more ideas, discuss each suggestion with the class, erasing those on which the class cannot reach a consensus. When the list is narrowed to three or four items, try either to combine the remaining ideas or to get a class consensus on one.

5. Follow through on the idea(s) by completing the project.

Discussion:

When might brainstorming be useful?

How could you do it by yourself, without pencil or paper?

How is it helpful to defer judgment on ideas?

Four-square Ideas

Grades K–3

Materials: drawing paper, crayons, sticker stars

Procedure:

1. Have the children fold their papers into quarters and then open them up.

2. Give them a clearly defined conflict problem. Have them illustrate four possible win-win solutions, one per square. Older children should also label their pictures. Younger children can dictate labels to you.

3. Have the children share their ideas. Give each child a star to stick on the picture of the idea he or she likes best.

Most children can come up with three or four ideas. Reassure those (if any) who cannot. Even one idea is better than none.

Discussion:

What were some of your ideas?

Which do you like best? Why?

Was it easy or hard to think up ideas?

How do you think up ideas?

What makes thinking up ideas easy or hard?

It's against the Law

Grades 2–6

Procedure:

1. Describe to the children a conflict situation. Have them write a definition of the problem and one possible action to resolve it.

2. Tell the class, "Sorry, the response you just gave is against the law; you can't use it. What else could you do in that situation?" Have the children write down another way to resolve it.

3. Continue until each child has developed four or five possible solutions. Point out that this was probably more than they thought they could come up with.

Discussion:

What helps you think of ideas?

Do you ever get stuck trying to think of ideas?

Did hearing "it's against the law" help you to get unstuck? Why?

Blockbusting

Here are some techniques to teach students to use when they face problems that are especially resistant to solution—when their minds are blocked, in other words.

1. *Picture it.* Have students picture mentally what the situation would look like if the problem were already solved. Have them imagine what the participants would do once a conflict were resolved. Have them then keep that image fixed mentally, asking themselves how they might get to that point from where they are.

2. *Wait.* Declare a moratorium on the problem for a specific period of time (more than half an hour). Assure students that they will return to the problem, but explain that for now they need a break.

3. *Change perspective.* Have students in conflict reverse roles, or go even further, asking "How would a bird in a tree view this conflict? How would a Martian view it? How would the floor you're standing on view it?"

4. *Think silly.* Have students come up with completely ridiculous solutions, the funnier and farther out the better. Once they've had a few laughs, they will have a surprisingly clearer perspective on the whole problem.

Strategy Skills

Children are often eager to help friends resolve disputes. One student I had—let's call him Steven—was not particularly aggressive or hostile, and yet nearly every day he was involved in a fight. I couldn't understand why until I began to notice a pattern. Steven never started the fight. He was always defending someone else, usually the person he perceived to be the underdog. Steven to the rescue! Unfortunately, he didn't know any nonviolent means of resolving the conflicts, and so every day he was in a fight. Like adults, children do better at creative conflict resolution if they have some techniques at their disposal.

Many of the conflict resolution techniques discussed in chapter two can be taught to students; you are the best judge of their applicability to your class. Activities for teaching mediating and negotiating are described here. More suggestions for teaching specific conflict resolution strategies are included in the Practice section of this chapter.

Conflict Resolution Chart

Grades K–6

Materials: chart paper, marking pen or crayon

Procedure:

1. Post a blank chart, headed *Conflict Resolution Techniques*. Explain that techniques will be listed on the chart as the children learn them. Try not to add to the chart too quickly. Be sure the students understand a technique thoroughly before moving to the next one.

2. You may want to add a new chart later, labeled *Not Recommended*, on which to note such tactics as fighting, hitting, tattling, and running away. The point here is that such modes of behavior are possible conflict resolution techniques, just not very good ones.

Taking Turns

Grades K–3

Materials: pennies, or materials with which to make a disk for flipping

Procedure:

1. Give each child a penny. Demonstrate, in case they don't know, how to flip it and how to read heads or tails.

2. You can make a class flipper out of corrugated cardboard or linoleum. The material needs to be heavy enough to flip well (a paper plate won't work). Label the sides *One* and *Two*. Punch a hole in the flipper and hang it in an accessible place. This will spare you from constantly being hit up for coins.

Discussion:

When might you need to flip a coin?

How would it help to resolve conflicts?

How would it help to prevent conflicts?

Negotiating

Grades 2–6

Procedure:

1. Write "Negotiate" and "Negotiating" on the board and have the class read them aloud. Ask if anyone knows what the words mean.

2. Explain that negotiating is a way of solving problems between people so that everyone can win.

3. List the following steps on the board:

   1. Say what you think the problem is.

   2. Say what you want.

   3. Say what the limits are.

   4. Work out an agreement.

   5. Ask if everyone is happy.

4. Walk the children through the steps with the following situation: Kevin keeps calling David "Fatso" and other names. David breaks Kevin's pencils and crayons.

Discussion:

In what kinds of situations would you want to negotiate?

How would you ask the other person to do it?

What if he or she won't?

What problems can you see arising during negotiating?

🍎 Negotiating is a skill kids will use the rest of their lives. Here are some situations I have used to give practice in different content areas. Once you're alert to the possibilities, many more situations will suggest themselves.

Math

There are five kids and fourteen cookies. Negotiate a fair way to share the cookies.

A used bike costs fifty dollars. You don't want to pay that much. Bargain.

Social Studies

You are white settlers who want to deal fairly with Native Americans during a land transaction. Set up an agreement that will allow you to live in peace.

As your town grows, some people say it must have a new sewer system. Others think that its construction will be too expensive and will tear up the streets for too long. Work it out.

Science

You are a family of ducks, similar to those in *Make Way for Ducklings.* Find a way to agree on a place to live.

The paper mill provides employment for the town, but its waste is polluting the river and killing wildlife. Negotiate an agreement between environmentalists and the company.

The peace team card samples (see Appendix) describe more hypothetical situations that could be used for negotiation practice.

Mediating

Grades 2–6

Procedure:

1. Ask the students what they would do if two friends were fighting. Elicit several suggestions, some of which will probably involve mediation, although the students aren't likely to recognize it as such.

2. Explain that mediating is trying to help people resolve a conflict. The mediator doesn't say who's right or wrong; she or he just helps the people find a solution that makes everyone happy.

3. Write the following steps on the board:

   1. Stay neutral.

   2. Give everyone a chance to talk.

   3. Think of ways to solve the problem.

   4. Find the solution everyone likes.

   Explain and discuss each of the steps.

4. Walk the students through the process with the following situation: Clara borrowed Jean's basketball and put a hole in it. Jean is now going to break something of Clara's.

5. Give lots of practice. As with negotiation, let students practice with situations taken from different content areas.

You might like to establish a classroom mediation project. Establish the criteria for becoming a classroom mediator, set up a training procedure, and certify mediators the way community mediation centers do.

Acting

No conflict resolution technique is any good without action. Students need to learn how to choose a possible solution to a conflict and act on the choice. This can be tricky. We want children to act, but not impulsively. They need to make a decision, consider the consequences, overcome any inhibitions they have, and plan how they will implement their decision. That's a tall order, even for adults. Consistent, gentle reminders to weigh consequences and plan actions are probably the most effective approach here. The hope is that students will begin to make the whole process a habit.

This skill of acting is perhaps the most difficult to separate from the others involved in conflict resolution. Therefore, once the kids start learning to develop potential solutions to conflict problems, always make it a point to ask what the first step would be toward their practical enactment.

Consequence Cards

Grades K–6

Materials: consequence cards (see below)

Procedure:

1. In advance, make consequence cards appropriate for your students' grade level by writing on three-by-five-inch index cards statements such as the following.

   K–3

   Janet leaves the house without her key.

   Andy borrows his brother's ball glove without asking.

   Tom's older brother forgets to put gas in the car.

   Anita and Sam build their block tower on the rug, not on the floor.

   4–6

   Jack tells everyone that he heard Steve's parents fighting when he was visiting there.

   Fran tells how she saw Rachel get spanked by her mother.

   Amy looks through Carmelita's desk without asking, trying to find a pencil sharpener.

2. In small groups, have children draw a card, read it (or hand it to you to read), and then describe a possible consequence of the action. Ask what other consequences might be.

Discussion:

Why is it important to think of consequences?

What might happen if you didn't?

First Steps

Grades 2–6

Materials: first steps worksheet (see Appendix)

Procedure:

Have the students complete the first steps worksheet.

Discussion:

What were the first steps you wrote?

Why would it be helpful to think in terms of first steps?

What might be different first steps for solving the same problems?

This Is How . . .

Grades 4–6

Materials: this is how . . . worksheet (see Appendix)

Procedure:

Distribute the this is how . . . worksheet. Students can work individually or in pairs. Discuss the responses.

Discussion:

How did you respond to the situations?

Did other people respond differently?

What was the most difficult situation for you to respond to?

Practice

Learning to respond creatively to conflict requires practice. The habits of aggression and passivity can be broken only when children have had experience with new approaches to conflict resolution.

There are two types of practice I recommend here. One is utilizing teachable moments, those times when conflicts occur under your nose. On these occasions, you can help children see that creative conflict resolution works in real situations and is superior to violent resolutions. Sometimes, however, real-life situations are too threatening or too intense to allow you to focus on the procedure of a conflict resolution technique. This is why structured practice sessions are valuable. They give students opportunities to practice in nonthreatening circumstances, to learn from mistakes, and to experiment with new ways of behaving.

Teachable Moments

Any teacher knows that often the best learning opportunities are not planned but spontaneous. This is as true for peacemaking as for any other subject. The peacemaking techniques you teach will have more meaning to students when they see them applied to real situations.

However, there is an art to taking advantage of teachable moments. Any time a conflict arises in your classroom, any time a student brings a conflict to you, there is potential for learning. First decide whether or not it is an appropriate time for teaching. As I discussed in chapters two and three, not all conflicts are appropriate for public resolution. Some are too threatening to the students; some, too personal in nature; and some, too complicated to unravel before an entire class. (And we might as well admit it: some are too boring to hold everyone's attention.) If you decide that it is a conflict good for public resolution, keep the following points in mind:

1. Whatever conflict resolution technique you use, name it. If the class is unfamiliar with it, explain the procedure.

2. Analyze the conflict with the class. Ask, "What is the problem? What can we do? What do we choose to do?"

3. Stress the search for a win-win solution.

4. Analyze the results of the conflict. Ask, "Did anything positive result? How else might the problem have been handled initially? Could it have been prevented?"

Structured Practice

Many of the activities in this chapter involve the use of hypothetical situations. A good source of these is the children themselves. Have them write descriptions of conflicts and drop them in a conflict box. Stress the importance of their recording who was involved and when, where, and why the conflict took place.

Role Playing

Grades 3–6

Procedure:

1. The procedure for role playing is described in chapter two. Role playing in practice sessions provides a safe way for children to try new types of behavior. You can also spend more time than is suggested in chapter two to discuss the role play, redo it if there is interest, and jointly analyze the children's response in depth.

2. Role plays will be more successful the more you keep the dramatic action moving along and use situations of high interest to the kids. If your school is equipped for videotaping, record some role-play sessions. Players and nonplayers will find the playback enlightening.

3. The following questions are useful for discussing role plays. (Remember that not all are appropriate to particular role plays or players.)

Discussion:

What was the conflict?

How was it resolved?

Was it a win-win resolution?

Will any positive changes happen as a result of this conflict resolution?

Could other solutions have worked?

How could the situation have been prevented?

How did the players feel in their roles?

How did these feelings affect their actions?

Hassle Lines

Grades 2–6

Procedure:

This is a variation of role play that was briefly described in chapter two during the discussion of role reversals.

1. Have the students form two lines, with each student facing a partner. Everyone in one line is person A, and everyone in the other line is person B.

2. Describe to the group a conflict situation involving two people, A and B. Explain that the group will play roles en masse until you shout "Freeze," at which point they will stop moving and talking.

3. Let the hassle line enact the role play for a few minutes (better too briefly than for too long). Cry, "Freeze!" At this point, you can continue the role play, reverse roles, discuss the results, or simply start a new role play.

● Hassle lines are noisy and confusing, but kids love them. They are a very good way for a group to loosen up and to practice role-play skills, and they are a good way to get shy students to participate.

Quick Decisions

Grades (K, 1), 2–6

Procedure:

Conflicts can flare up and go out of control quickly. Because children won't always have time to think out responses carefully, they need practice in formulating effective responses on the spot. This technique gives them that practice.

1. Begin by using either conventional role play or the hassle line. Freeze the role play.

2. Give the players thirty to sixty seconds to come up with a resolution to the conflict. Emphasize speed.

3. Evaluate the resolutions.

Discussion:

What kinds of resolutions did you come up with?

Are they win-win resolutions?

Do they effectively solve the problem?

What was it like having to think so fast?

Can you think of any situation in which you might have to think fast?

Why should you be careful when you do?

What should you be careful about when you do?

Role Reversals

Grades 2–6

Procedure:

Role reversals, explained in chapter two, can be used with conventional role plays and hassle lines. It is one of the most effective ways to teach peacemaking skills.

Skits

Grades 2–6

Procedure:

Skits are a structured kind of role play, and they don't carry the threat that role playing sometimes does. They are fun and make excellent discussion starters.

1. Meet with a small group of kids. Present or develop with the group a conflict situation to use as the basis of the skit. Discuss and develop the parts and lines. Provide opportunities to rehearse.

2. Have the group present the skit to the class. Freeze the skit at the point of conflict. Request solutions to the problem, and discuss them with actors and audience. The actors can try to respond in character to the suggestions.

3. If the actors have worked out their own solution, they can present it and then discuss it with the class.

● Older children often enjoy developing and presenting skits to younger ones. If an older student is capable, he or she can freeze the skit and lead the discussion, or you can teach the technique ahead of time to the younger children's teacher. Skits also can be videotaped for this use.

Puppets

Grades K–3, (4–6)

Procedure:

Many of the techniques you use with people you can use with puppets. In chapter two, I discussed role play with the problem puppets. Puppets also can be used in the skit format above. Young children enjoy the following procedure:

1. Give each child a puppet. Present a short skit involving a conflict between two puppets. Freeze the action at the point of conflict.

2. Have each child find a partner. Have the partners use their puppets to make a quick-decision resolution. Choose a few partners to present these to the class.

3. Present a new situation, and repeat the procedure, having different sets of children present solutions. (This approach maintains interest longer than having all the children present solutions to a single conflict.)

Critical Incidents[2]

Grades K–6

Procedure:

Critical incidents are short, open-ended stories that present children with a moral dilemma. In thinking through possible solutions to these dilemmas, children are required to integrate the basic skills of conflict resolution. The stories can be used to spark discussion on a number of issues, moral and otherwise; but here are three, for three different grade levels, that deal with conflict.

Grade K
Angela was walking home from school. In a vacant lot she saw two big girls throwing stones at a dog. She wanted to help the puppy, but she was afraid of the big girls.

What's the problem here?

What could Angela do?

Why might the big girls throw stones at the puppy?

What should happen to the big girls?

Has anything like this happened to you?

Grade 3

Amy is very interested in dinosaurs. She is so interested in dinosaurs that she reads nothing but books about dinosaurs. When she has to write in school, it's usually about dinosaurs; and she sometimes skips her homework to work on her dinosaur collection. Today Mr. Rosenberg found her reading a dinosaur book instead of doing her math, and he said she could not do anything with dinosaurs ever again in class.

How do you think Amy feels?

What's the problem here?

If you were Mr. Rosenberg, what would you do?

If you were Amy, how would you try to get Mr. Rosenberg to change his mind?

Grade 6

Denise is an emotionally disturbed child who has been main-streamed. She gets easily frightened and cries and screams when she does. Because of her unusual behavior, the other kids have made her an outcast. This has increased her fears and made her behavior worse.

Why would the kids ostracize Denise?

What's the problem here?

Who could change things?

What could the teacher do?

What could you do in this situation?

How would you start?

Writing and Drawing Activities

Reversed Fairy Tales

Grades 3–6   Materials: pencils, paper

Procedure:

Have the children rewrite fairy tales (such as "The Three Bears") from the point of view of the antagonist. Have them portray the antagonist sympathetically. Kids get a big kick out of these reversed stories, and they can form the basis of very funny skits as well.

Picture Books

Grades (K, 1), 2–6   Materials: pencils, paper, crayons

Procedure:

Have students write stories of conflicts with win-win resolutions in a picture-book format, i.e., a few sentences per page with illustrations. Students who don't like to draw can team up with students who do. Share the finished stories with younger students. Young children can dictate stories and then illustrate them.

Comic Strips

Grades 2–6

Materials: large drawing paper, crayons

Procedure:
Have students fold large sheets of drawing paper into eighths. Then describe several conflict situations and have the students choose one on which to base a comic strip showing steps to a possible win-win solution. Assure them that stick figures are perfectly all right.

I have found this activity to be very successful, even with second graders. I repeat it during the year, having the kids think up their own conflict situations. Sometimes I describe to them conflicts in space or another fantastic setting instead of real-life situations.

Children's Books

Grades K–6

Materials: pencils, paper

Procedure:
Since conflict is basic to the plot in most fiction, children's books are a good source of discussion or writing topics.

1. Stop reading at the point of conflict and ask, "What is the conflict? How do you think it will be resolved? How would you resolve it?"

2. Finish reading the story. Ask, "How was the conflict resolved? Was it like or unlike our suggestion? Was it an effective, win-win resolution? What would you have done differently?"

3. If the resolution presented is really terrible, have the students write new endings and display them on a bulletin board.

How conflicts are handled in books, and how teachers in turn handle those books, is a sensitive issue. There is a big difference, I feel, between discussing alternate endings with kids and changing the ending of a book yourself. The former is an exercise in creativity and critical thinking; the latter is censorship. Rather than censor, better confront the issues that disturb you in a book. For example, if a book is sexist, have the children identify the elements that make it sexist. Ask them how they would change it. Ask, "Why does it make a difference?" Finally, if a book is really offensive, simply don't use it at all.

Superheroes for Peace

Grades 2–6

Materials: drawing paper, crayons, scissors, paste, large paper for mounting, writing paper, pencils

Procedure:
1. Have students work in groups of three or four. Explain that the task of each group is to develop a superhero or superheroes who resolve conflicts nonviolently.

2.   Students should draw pictures of their superheroes and cut out and mount the drawings on display paper. They should also write down:

   1.   the superhero's name

   2.   what power she or he has

   3.   how she or he resolves conflicts

   4.   other interesting information

Discussion:

How does your superhero resolve conflicts?

How did you get your ideas?

Do you resolve conflicts the same way?

I first did this project with a third grade group. I expected that the superheroes would resolve conflicts using the techniques we had talked about in class. They didn't. Instead, they resolved conflicts by using laser beams, Z rays, and complicated machinery. Creative as the results were, I wasn't sure the kids were getting the point.

I mentioned this to the class. One of the kids explained patiently that *anyone* could use negotiation, mediation, and similar techniques. These were superheroes, so they had to use very special techniques for resolving conflicts.

I have since found that most students, regardless of age, think this way. And that's fine—they are still learning that nonviolent conflict resolution is important enough for even a superhero.

Incidentally, this has been one of the most successful activities I've ever used. Kids can, and usually do, take off with it. The following two activities were inspirations of kids with whom I have worked.

Supervillains

Grades 2–6

Materials: drawing paper, crayons, scissors, paste, large paper for mounting, writing paper, pencils

Procedure:

Once superheroes are created, students may want to develop supervillains who go around starting conflicts. Use the same procedure as for superheroes.

Discussion:

How does your supervillain start conflicts?

Is that how real conflicts get started?

What would you do if you met your supervillain?

Superhero Comics

Grades 2–6

Materials: drawing paper, pencils, crayons

Procedure:

Once superheroes have been invented, have students show you what the heroes can do by writing and drawing comic strips of their adventures.

They can do this before supervillains are invented, of course, but the villains add spice.

🍎 I have also had students who used superheroes for peace in skits, dioramas, statues, and radio plays (over the PA system).

Design a Peace Toy

Grades 2–6

Materials: pencils, paper, crayons

Procedure:

1. Discuss what violent and nonviolent toys and games are. List on the board the violent toys and games the kids can think of.

2. Have the class work in groups or individually to redesign a violent toy or game or invent a new toy or game with a peace motif. Display the finished designs.

Discussion:

Why is it important to have toys and games with peace themes?

What problems can you see with war toys?

Is it all right to play war?

What were some of the problems you encountered in redesigning your toy or game?

Learning about the UN

Grades 3–6

Procedure:

As the United Nations is the major peacekeeping body in the world today, it's valuable for students to understand how it works. It can also be used as a springboard topic for an enormous amount of learning, as suggested below. UN day is October 24, but don't worry if it's gone by. I always wait until my class has a grasp of conflict and conflict resolution before I begin.

1. Divide the class into groups of four. Assign each group an aspect of the UN such as organization, jobs of each body, or projects undertaken. Have the groups research and prepare oral reports for the class. Or all your students might pool their findings and write up a guide to the United Nations. (Another alternative is the jigsaw groups approach described in chapter seven.)

2. Once the class understands how the UN works, have them role-play a meeting of the general assembly. This can be very elaborate if you desire. Assign a different country for each student to research and then represent at a mock general assembly. Also teach the basics of parliamentary procedure. Have the class look into the issues facing the UN and choose one to debate.

World Flag

Grades 2–6

Materials: pictures of flags of various nations, picture of UN flag, twelve-by-twenty-four-inch tagboard, crayons

Procedure:

1. Discuss flags, what they represent, and how people feel about them.

2. Have students design a flag to symbolize peace and world unity. Have them draw their flags on large tagboard. Hang the flags about the room.

Discussion:

What kinds of symbols did you think about for your flag?

How did you choose the symbols you used?

Peace Symbols

Grades 2–6

Materials: pictures of peace symbols (e.g., dove, UN symbol)

Procedure:

Show students common peace symbols and discuss their meaning. Have them design their own symbols and write paragraphs explaining what they included in the symbols and why.

Discussion:

What are symbols used for?

How else do people express feelings about peace?

Where might you use a peace symbol? (Emphasize, not to deface public property.)

Give students sheets of white stickers on which to copy their symbols.

"I Have a Dream" Revisited

Grades 4–6

Materials: recording and written text of Martin Luther King, Jr.'s "I Have a Dream" speech.

Procedure:

1. Play the recording and read the text of the "I Have a Dream" speech. Discuss the vision of peace and equality it reflects. Relate this to conflict resolution.

2. Have students write their own versions of the speech and share them with the class. Emphasize that the speeches should focus on the student's dreams for the world and its people.

Discussion:

What does King's vision of the world have to do with what we've learned about conflict?

How is your dream speech like and unlike his?

Why did you choose the themes you chose for your dream speech?

How could you make the dream you spoke of come true?

Other Activities for Writing and Drawing

Many of the activities described in this and other chapters either are, or can be adapted to, writing and drawing activities. Among them are:

Conflict Scripts	Historical Cooperation
Critical Incidents	It's against the Law
Four-square Ideas	Puppets
Historical Conflicts	Skits

Notes

1. Susan Carpenter, *A Repertoire of Peacemaking Skills* (Consortium on Peace Research, Education and Development, 1977).

2. For a more complete discussion, I recommend James Hoffman, *Critical Incidents* (Brimingham, Mich.: Instructional Fair, 1972).

Chapter 5

Improving Communication Skills

Several years ago in a teachers' lounge, I overheard a conversation that went something like this:

Louise: You know, Irene is a little upset with you.

Helen: With me? Why?

Louise: She says you were very rude to her this morning.

Helen: I haven't even talked to her today!

Louise: That's what she said. You passed her in the hall without saying a word.

Helen: I had to get to the office to duplicate a letter for parents. I didn't really notice her. Well, I'll go explain things. . . . That is, if she's still speaking to *me*.

All conflict resolution involves communication. This is not to suggest that communication in and of itself is a panacea. When it comes to conflict, we usually do not need more communication; we need better communication. Communication is a double-edged sword in conflict resolution. It can escalate or de-escalate a conflict depending on how it is used. To understand this dual role, it's necessary to understand the complete process of communication.

Conflict is largely a perceived phenomenon. It is our perception of a situation that tells us it is, or is not, a conflict. Keeping that in mind, let's look at the communication process.

First, there is an *observation*. Your senses register that something is happening. Then what is observed is *perceived*. You interpret, through various filters (such as your values, needs, and experience), what is going on in what you've just observed. Next you *encode* what you've interpreted by formulating it into speech and gesture. Then you *transmit* it. Once transmitted, the message is *received* and *decoded*. The listener's senses register the input and sort it out. Then it is *perceived* as the listener understands and interprets the message through perceptual filters.

We tend to be most aware of the transmission and reception aspects of communication. Our lack of awareness of the roles of observation and perception fuels conflict in our lives. It is from misobservation and misperception that many conflicts arise.

Here's what the process looks like all together:

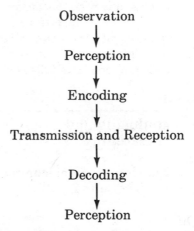

In conflict situations, our perception of what we see or hear tells us whether or not we think there are threats to our wants, needs, or values. Then we act or react, based on that perception. As the model above shows, the process of communication is much the same. In the anecdote at the beginning of the chapter, Irene perceived Helen's indifference as a threat, perhaps to her need to be liked. She responded by labeling Helen's behavior as rudeness. She also ceased communicating directly with Helen, opting instead to communicate via Louise. (A very risky option, incidentally. There were no guarantees that Louise would act as an effective go-between. If she had chosen to do nothing, or to gossip, the conflict would have escalated further.) Helen chose to reopen the communication and to clarify Irene's perceptions, thus resolving the conflict.

As this one incident shows, awareness of the entire communication process is important to resolving conflict. Even if we are aware, however, communication still is not inherently helpful. Communication can always cause a conflict to escalate, and this frequently happens when people fall into what I call communication potholes.

Communication potholes are any behavior forms that can make a conflict situation worse, usually by confusing it or making everyone involved more defensive. Factors that confuse a conflict situation are:

displaying emotional excitement

injecting too many unnecessary facts

jumping to conclusions or making assumptions

not listening or interrupting

Factors that contribute to defensiveness are:

using authoritarian tactics

condescending

using loaded words

flaunting power

There are many other factors that lead to confusion or defensiveness, as I'm sure you know. The important thing to keep in mind is that to change a conflict situation from dysfunctional to functional requires an awareness of the effect of what you communicate. The communication must clarify the situation and make the people involved feel important and dignified. This is, of course, the ideal. In actual practice, communication in conflicts falls somewhere on this continuum:

1	5	10
confusing and threatening		clarifying and safe

The closer the communication is to ten, the more smoothly the conflict will be resolved.

Improving Communication Skills for Conflict Resolution

If we want to improve communication for conflict resolution in our classrooms, we need to help students improve the following skills:

1. observing
2. being aware of perception and what affects it
3. transmitting accurately
4. listening carefully and clarifying perceptions
5. understanding communication blocks

As it happens, time spent on these communications skills is very well spent indeed, for they have obvious uses in areas other than conflict resolution. In fact, you should aim at making good communication habits second nature to your students.

But before we talk about the children, let's talk about you and me. As teachers, we are the ones who establish a climate that is conducive to effective communication and the ones who model good communication behavior. You are probably doing a great deal in this area already. Try the following exercises to determine if you're touching some important bases.

Exercise

Read the statements. Do they reflect your behavior often, sometimes, or never?

1. I look children in the eyes when listening to them.
2. I try to paraphrase what the kids say when I don't understand.
3. I don't repeat children's answers.
4. I give praise only when it is deserved.
5. I redirect questions from kids back to the class, rather than answering myself.
6. I describe behavior in nonjudgmental ways.
7. I share some personal information about myself with the kids.
8. I avoid saying one thing with words and another with my body.
9. I wait at least five seconds for children's answers before I prompt them.
10. I don't interrupt.
11. I say "please," "thank you," and "excuse me" when talking to children.

Behaving a certain way is the first step in getting your students to act that way. This can't be overemphasized. All the preceding statements reflect behavior that helps improve the classroom communication climate:

1. Looking children in the eyes is a nonverbal cue that you are listening.
2. Paraphrasing (listening reflectively) shows that you care enough about what the child is saying to get it right.
3. If you don't repeat their answers, the kids are required to speak loudly and clearly the first time.
4. Teachers often praise automatically. The insincerity is detected by the children, and the teacher's praise loses its power of reward.
5. Redirecting questions back to the class shows that you want them to talk to each other, not just to you.
6. Describing behavior in nonjudgmental ways demonstrates your openness to hearing a child's view of things.

7. Sharing some personal information about yourself builds an atmosphere of trust and encourages kids to open up.

8. Body language that does not contradict your verbal language shows your sincerity.

9. Waiting at least five seconds gives kids a chance to answer and indicates that you really want to hear what they have to say.

10. Your not interrupting implies that you think what the kids say is important. It fosters politeness, too.

11. Saying "please," "thank you," and "excuse me" also fosters politeness.

As you yourself act in ways that improve communication, it doesn't hurt to point out your behavior to the students occasionally. Let them know that you are conscious of what you are doing.

Try in the lessons that follow to relate the learning to the children's lives whenever possible. This will lead to the most lasting improvement in their skills.

Activities are described in this chapter under the following headings:

Observation and Perception

Improving Listening and Transmission

Recognizing Communication Barriers

Nonverbal Communication

Other Communication in the Classroom

Observation and Perception

The activities described below are designed to help students learn to observe more carefully and to increase their understanding of perception. Help your students see the connections between perception and conflict. This awareness of perception and the factors that influence it will aid them in understanding conflict and learning to resolve it.

Eyewitness Accounts

Grades K–6

Procedure:

1. At odd moments during the day, stop everything unexpectedly, and say, "Time for an eyewitness account."

2. Ask for a volunteer or two to give an account of what just occurred or what was just said in the room. Ask other class members to add to or correct the account.

3. Follow the same procedure when showing a movie or filmstrip with action. Switch off the projector and ask what was just going on or being said.

🍎 Avoid the temptation to use this as a way to catch inattentive students. Rather, use it as a spontaneous and enjoyable exercise for rewarding careful observation.

Eyewitness Skits

Grades K–6

Procedure:

1. With a small group, develop and rehearse a skit. The skit should contain lots of details relative to the action.

2. Have the children present the skit to the rest of the class. Call on several volunteers to summarize what happened in the skit. The accounts will vary.

Discussion:

What details did you notice?

What details did you miss?

Why did people notice certain things and not others?

What would help you be more observant?

Changes 1, 2, 3

Grades K–6

Procedure:

1. Have the students work in pairs. Student A should carefully examine student B for thirty seconds and turn around.

2. Student B should then change three aspects of his or her appearance, e.g., cross the arms differently, take a watch off.

3. Student A tries to guess what B changed. Then student B observes, and student A changes.

Discussion:

What made this game easy or hard?

Did it get easier the more you did it?

Optical Illusions

Grades K–6

Materials: optical illusion pictures

Procedure:

Show the pictures one at a time and discuss.

Discussion:

What do you see here?

Does anyone see anything different?

How can two people looking at the same picture see such different things?

Why do some things appear to be what they're not?

Have you ever had an experience in which you thought you saw something, but it wasn't there?

Parts and Wholes

Grades **K–3, (4–6)**

Materials: pictures from magazines, cardboard, construction paper, tape

Procedure:

1. Mount several pictures on separate pieces of cardboard. Set construction paper over each picture and attach with tape hinges so that the construction paper can be lifted. Cut a hole in the construction paper so that all of the picture will be covered except one (highly intriguing) part.

2. Have students write or discuss what they think each picture is about on the basis of the part they see.

🍎 Older children enjoy this activity more than you might think. They particularly enjoy preparing the pictures and trying to fool others.

Discussion:

What could you accurately say about this picture on the basis of what you see here?

What can't you say?

What does *context* mean?

Why is it important to get the whole picture of a conflict situation?

Different Angles

Grades **K–6**

Materials: drawing paper, crayons

Procedure:

Have students fold paper into thirds. Ask them to choose something to draw and to draw it from three different angles (for instance, from above, from the front, and from below). Display the drawings.

Discussion:

Why do things look different from different angles?

Why do different people see things differently?

How would that affect what they do?

How might that lead to conflict?

The Martian Viewpoint

Grades **3–6**

Materials: pencils, paper

Procedure:

Have students write a description of a typical classroom activity from the point of view of a Martian who has never seen it before. Have volunteers read their descriptions to the class.

🍎 Kids have a lot of fun with this activity, and it can be repeated many times.

Discussion:

What assumptions do we make about other people's points of view?

Why aren't those assumptions necessarily valid?

How might those assumptions contribute to misunderstanding?

What factors influence one's point of view?

People Perceive Differently

Grades (1, 2), 3–6

Materials: pictures

Procedure:

1. Show the class a picture and ask them to list three things that are important (or interesting) about it.

2. Have the students rank order their observations from most important to least important (or from most interesting to least interesting).

3. Have them share their lists. Remind them that there are no right or wrong answers. Point out not only that different people saw different things, but that they felt different things were important or interesting.

Discussion:

What details did you feel were most important?

What influences decisions about importance?

🍎 With younger children, simply show the pictures and discuss what are important details in them.

Perception and Frame of Reference[1]

Grades 3–6

Procedure:

1. Ask students to agree or disagree with the following:

—— is the best school in town.

The United States is the best country to live in.

The Yankees are the best baseball team.

The recent test in —— was easy.

Record the numbers of those who agree and disagree on the board.

2. Explain that their answers are in part the result of their *frames of reference*, which reflect their values, beliefs, experiences, and upbringing.

3. Return to each statement and discuss it.

Discussion:

Did you believe this? Why? Why not?

What influenced this belief?

What would a student from another school or country believe?

What would influence him or her in this belief?

How would your frame of reference differ from his or hers?

🍎 As an extension, pair students off. Have them list three things that contribute to their sharing a frame of reference, and three things that contribute to their having different frames of reference.

A Typical Day

Grades 3–6

Materials: pencils, paper

Procedure:

1. Discuss with the class a typical school day, writing a schedule on the board.

2. Have students write a description of the day from their own points of view. Then have them rephrase the descriptions to reflect your point of view.

🍎 This activity not only gives practice in paraphrasing and looking from different perspectives, it also can reveal how students view you.

Discussion:

How are the two points of view the same?

How are they different?

Why do students and teachers have different points of view?

How might that lead to conflict?

How do you handle conflicts with your teacher?

Jumping to Conclusions

Grades 1–3

Procedure:

1. Explain the term *jumping to conclusions*. Read descriptions similar to these, asking why:

   Janet is crying. Why?

   Jeffrey isn't talking to Amos. Why?

   Harriet just hit Freddy. Why?

   Dana is laughing at Jerome. Why?

   Abe is ignoring Judy. Why?

   Have the children volunteer possible conclusions. Before they state a conclusion, they should jump two or three feet forward.

2. Ask if anyone can think of another conclusion. Have that person jump before he or she contributes. Solicit at least two possible conclusions for each situation.

Discussion:

What else do you need to know before you can draw an accurate conclusion?

How could you find out that information?

How might jumping to conclusions cause problems with others?

How might it affect a conflict?

Has anyone ever jumped to a conclusion about you?

⬤ Ergo, a more sophisticated version of this activity, can be used with older students (see chapter six).

Understanding Misunderstandings

Grades (K–2), 3–6

Procedure:

1. Ask, "What is a misunderstanding?" Discuss as suggested below.

2. Have the students use as ideas the situations they just recounted:

> to write a short story showing how a misunderstanding might be cleared up
>
> to make a comic strip
>
> to write and perform a puppet play for younger students
>
> to write a skit for the class

Discussion:

What was a misunderstanding you were involved in?

How did you feel about it?

How did the other person feel?

Did you clear it up? How?

What are some ways of clearing up misunderstandings?

⬤ With young children, omit step two and discuss misunderstandings, relating them to jumping to conclusions. You can use problem puppets to introduce this activity.

A Misunderstandings Flow Chart

Grades 3–6

Materials: pencils, drawing paper

Procedure:

1. Discuss the communication process and how misunderstandings occur.

2. Have students work in small groups to develop a flow chart of an imaginary conversation that includes a misunderstanding.

3. Have groups show flow charts to the rest of the class. Then develop a class flow chart on the board that diagrams the communication process, including misunderstandings, how they develop, and how they are resolved.

Discussion:

How can misunderstandings be resolved?

What do the flow charts show us about misunderstandings?

Improving Listening and Transmission

Since these are two skills on which teachers already spend much time and attention, I have included only a few activities, the ones I think are most useful in teaching children to respond to conflict. The technique of reflective listening is detailed in chapter two as a teacher's mediation strategy. Here it is presented as a technique older children can use. It will have more meaning to them if they understand the concepts of perception and misperception and the role they play in conflict.

Useful supplements in this area are any listening comprehension activities that require students to remember details, think about cause and effect, make predictions, or synthesize information, and any language arts activities that increase students' vocabularies, require them to give directions, or require them to speak in front of others.

How You Say It

Grades K-6

Procedure:

Voice pitch, volume, and clarity have an effect on conflict. High-pitched, shouting, or mumbling voices are abrasive and can escalate conflict. The following are voice exercises that students can try.

1. Speaking loudly without shouting is easy when you speak from the diaphragm. Show the children where their diaphragms are. Have them stand erect and place their hands on their diaphragms. Then ask them to say "Ho, ho, ho, ho, ho!" while concentrating on making the sound come from the diaphragm. Once they've accomplished this, have them say words and sentences while concentrating on making sound come from the diaphragm. Try also having the children participate in conversations standing across the room from each other, the object being to practice speaking loudly without shouting.

2. To practice enunciation, give the class a choral reading passage. As they read, have them enunciate each word in an exaggerated fashion. Repeat this exercise regularly to help students break the mumbling habit.

Discussion:

Why would speaking clearly be useful in resolving conflicts?

What effect might shouting or mumbling have on conflict?

Sifting for Five Ws

Grades (K-2), 3-6

Procedure:

1. Discuss what kinds of information people need to begin resolving conflicts. When one of the five-W words comes up in the discussion, write it on the board. Add those that don't come up.

2. Tell the class that you have a listening exercise and that they'll need to listen for the five Ws—who, what, when, where, and why. Read descriptions of several different conflict situations. Have the students identify the who, what, when, where, and why of each situation.

Discussion:

Which of the five-Ws were not present in this story?

How does their absence affect your perception of the situation?

 Young children can do this activity if you focus on only one or two five-W words at a time.

Summaries of Summaries

Grades 4—6

Materials: news stories involving conflicts, pencils, paper

Procedure:

1. Have students bring in news stories involving conflicts, and then have them write short paragraphs summarizing the stories. Remind them to include the five Ws.

2. Have each student pass the completed story to a friend, who is to come up with a headline that more or less summarizes the story.

Discussion:

Did your headline writer accurately summarize your story?

Why is it important to be able to summarize accurately?

Good Listener Checklist

Grades 1–4, (5, 6)

Materials: good listener checklist (see Appendix)

Procedure:

Have the children fill out and discuss the good listener checklist. Repeat the exercise several times during the year, particularly after cooperation activities and an activity such as the positive focus game (presented later in this chapter).

Discussion:

Why is [*specific behavior from checklist*] important for good listening?

What are some situations in which you thought it was important to be a good listener?

Why would good listening be important in conflict?

 Have older students develop their own good listener checklists.

Pete and Repeat

Grades 2–6

Procedure:

1. Explain what paraphrasing is. Give the students some practice by helping them paraphrase the following:

It's very warm out today.

I saw some boring TV shows last night.

We're going to take an interesting field trip.

The book I'm reading now is exciting.

2. Have the students pair off. Designate one student as Pete and the other as Repeat. Explain that whenever Pete says something, he or she will stop for a moment, and Repeat will paraphrase it. Pete should nod or say "uh-huh" if it is an accurate paraphrase.

3. Have all the Petes talk about things they did this morning. After a few minutes, stop the activity and have the students switch roles. Then continue as above.

Discussion:

Was it easy or difficult to paraphrase accurately?

What problems did you encounter when you tried to paraphrase?

Can you see any advantages to paraphrasing in conversations?

Can you see any disadvantages?

Demonstrating Reflective Listening

Grades 2–6

Procedure:

1. Explain the procedure of reflective listening. Remind the class of their experiences in paraphrasing.

2. With another adult or a child, do a role play of a conflict involving a misunderstanding in which you listen reflectively to help resolve it.

3. Discuss the role play and reflective listening.

Discussion:

Will someone please explain the reflective listening procedure?

How did reflective listening clear up the misunderstanding?

What was the perception of person A? Person B?

Can you think of a situation in which you might use reflective listening?

You Sez, I Sez

Grades K–6

Procedure:

1. Have the class sit in a circle. One child should begin by making a statement such as "My favorite Saturday activity is ———."

2. The next child reflects this by saying, "You say you like to watch TV on Saturday; I say I like to visit my father." Continue around the circle, each child giving his or her opinion after reflecting the previous child's.

Positive Focus Game[2]

Grades K–6

Procedure:

1. Divide the class into groups of three. One child volunteers to be the focus person.

2. Give the class a topic such as:

Why I do or don't believe in ghosts.

Why I would or wouldn't like to go out in space.

The focus person then talks for two or three minutes about the topic. The other two children should listen (focus) carefully. They are allowed only to ask questions of the focus person, never to criticize or to disagree.

3. At the end, the two people try to remember what the focus person said and paraphrase it back to him or her.

Discussion:

How did the focus person feel?

Did the focus person do a good job of explaining?

What kinds of questions did you ask?

What other kinds of information did you need to draw out?

Did anyone want to express disagreement with the focus person? How did it feel not to do that?

Was it hard to really focus on the person for two or three minutes? How did you make yourself do that?

Recognizing Communication Barriers

As I said earlier in this chapter, if communication is going to resolve conflicts, not escalate them, then an awareness of the most and least effective ways of communicating is important. In the following activities, children learn both about barriers identified by research and about those barriers they can identify as relevant to their own lives.

Defensiveness

Grades 2-6

Procedure:

1. Write the word *defensive* on the board and define it. Relate it to its root, *defend*. Explain that when people get defensive, they are more interested in defending themselves than in resolving conflicts in a win-win manner.

2. Have the class close eyes and relax. Say, "Think about how you would feel if someone:

"called you stupid

"quietly started to take your things

"sneered at everything you said

"accused you of stealing when you didn't

"got lots of people to laugh when you walked by

"These situations might bring out many feelings, but one emotion that would probably be brought out in each is a defensive one, as if you needed to defend yourself against someone or something."

Discussion:

Have you ever felt defensive?

What made you feel that way?

How did the feeling go away?

Arguments and Discussions[3]

Grades 4–6

Procedure:

1. Ask students, "What is the difference between an argument and a discussion?" Note their ideas on the board. If they get stuck, ask, "What about tone of voice, body language, choice of words?" The chart may end up looking something like this:

Arguments	Discussions
Loud, angry, harsh tone of voice	Quiet, calm, even tone of voice
Interrupting	Letting other person finish a point before you start
Insults, put-downs, sarcasm	Respectfulness, friendliness
Exaggerations (terrible, evil, never, everybody, always)	Careful, exact words
Goal is to win	Goal is to find truth

2. Put practice topics on the board and ask for two volunteers to argue about and then discuss one of the topics on which they disagree.

Discussion:

How does an argument make you feel? A discussion?

Can you still be angry and have a discussion?

What are the benefits of discussing over arguing?

Loaded Words

Grades K–6

Procedure:

Brainstorm a list of loaded words, i.e., words that carry or elicit very emotional and unusually defensive reactions.

Discussion:

How would using these words in a conflict make you feel?

What would that do to the conflict?

What would you do if someone used them a lot?

This activity can be related to the put-downs activity (presented later in this chapter).

Potholes

Grades K–6

Procedure:

1. On the board list communication potholes, i.e., ways of acting that make the communication process more difficult. For example, you might note behavior that is bossy, superior, interrupting, putting down, absolutely sure, threatening, or sneaky.

2. Have students role-play or give examples of these ways of behaving.

3. Have students rank order the list from most annoying to least annoying.

Discussion:

Why is —— a communication pothole?

If you were in a conflict and someone started being ——, how would you feel?

What could you do to counteract it?

Which of these potholes annoys you the most?

What potholes did we forget?

Buzzer

Grades K–6

Procedure:

1. Once children have an awareness of communication potholes and loaded words, they are ready to start spotting them in situations.

2. Plan with a couple of students to present a role play of a conflict with lots of potholes and loaded words.

3. Whenever anyone perceives a loaded word or a pothole, he or she should leap up and say, "Buzz." Then the role play should continue.

Discussion:

What potholes and loaded words did we find?

How would they interfere with resolving the conflict?

What could the players do when they encounter them?

Nonverbal Communication

The idea of body language fascinates kids; and, indeed, the exploration of this relatively new field of nonverbal communication is fascinating. One author estimates that ninety percent of communication is nonverbal. While the percentage may be disputed, the fact remains that nonverbal communication is important.

Nonverbal communication is more than body language, although that is all I will address here. It includes such factors as arrangement of physical environment, dress, use of time, and pitch and modulation of voice. We will be focusing on the four factors that give the most additional information about what is being said: facial expression, posture, gestures, and intonation.

To facilitate conflict resolution, body language should reinforce the message that both parties are open and willing to talk and listen to one another. This is most clearly indicated by sitting or standing face to face. Hands should not gesticulate wildly, and each party should lean slightly toward the other. The parties should not be too close to each other, and they should look each other in the eye (although not in a hostile fashion).

If a person says she or he is willing to negotiate, but really isn't, this is often apparent in body language, e.g., nervous gestures and eye movements, body turning away, slight or overt facial grimaces. Children are especially open in displaying body cues.

Be careful how you interpret body language, however. It should be interpreted only in the context of the situation: most experts agree that, contrary to popular literature on the subject, specific movements rarely have specific meanings. For example, a crossed-arm stance may be a defensive posture. It may also be a stern one. Or it may mean the person is chilly. Ordinarily, body language will either generally support what is being said or obviously contradict it.

TV Body Language

Grades K–6

Materials: television set

Procedure:
Play a TV show with the volume turned off. Have the children guess what is being communicated by facial and body movements. After ten minutes or so, have them try to communicate various things using body language.

🍎 They may have a tendency to slip into pantomime. Discuss the difference.

Mirroring

Grades K–6

Procedure:
1. Have the pupils pair off and stand face to face. One person is A and the other is B.

2. Have all the As begin to move, slowly and smoothly. The Bs try to imitate their movements exactly. The As' object is to be imitated smoothly, not to trick the Bs.

3. After a few minutes, tell the Bs to lead the movement and have the As imitate.

4. Finish by having no one lead, simply having partners move together.

🍎 This is a good quieting-down and tension-releasing activity.

Body Listening

Grades 2–6

Procedure:
1. Have students get partners. Give them a topic, such as "What I'm doing after school."

2. Partners stand facing each other. A should talk about the topic while B listens and imitates all of A's body and facial movements. After a few minutes, have them change roles.

Discussion:

Who was easy to talk to? Difficult?

What made them easy or difficult to talk to?

Who was easy or difficult to listen to? Why?

What was it like having someone copy all your movements?

Intonation

Grades 2–6

Procedure:

1. Write on the board "Go to the office now" without any ending punctuation. Ask for volunteers to read the sentence aloud in ways that change the meaning:

Go to the *office* now.   (not somewhere else)

Go to the office *now*!   (this minute)

Go to the *office now*!   (you're in trouble)

2. Discuss intonation and how it can affect meaning. have students think of sentences that have different meanings depending upon intonation, for instance:

We fed her puppy biscuits.

The rumor that Harry and Bob made up was false.

Discussion:

How is meaning carried by more than just words?

How could intonation cause a misunderstanding?

How could you prevent such a misunderstanding?

Other Communication in the Classroom

We have talked almost exclusively about communication as it relates to classroom conflict. I also want to talk about two other kinds of classroom communication.

One form is classroom discussion. Discussions can be wonderful learning experiences, or they can be boring. Since creative conflict resolution often depends on discussion, the topic is worth, if you'll pardon the expression, discussing.

Here are some tips for getting a good discussion going. Have everyone seated so they can see each other. This encourages students to talk to each other, not just to you.

Begin with an open-ended, challenging event or activity. This gives the kids something to talk about. From the activities you've seen so far, it must be obvious that I favor giving kids some kind of active experience from which they can draw conclusions. You can also begin with a film-strip, a story, an unfinished sentence, a role play, a game, or whatever will grab interest. The object of the discussion is not to elicit right answers; make this clear to the students and then be supportive of the responses you get.

Keep the discussion moving along, and structure it so that everyone can participate painlessly. Going around the circle, drawing names from a hat, working in pairs—all these encourage everyone's involvement. (You should, however, give the kids the option to pass.)

Encourage the kids to respond to each other. You might want to try this adaptation of You Sez, I Sez: before any student can contribute to the discussion, he or she must summarize what the previous speaker said.

When the children ask questions of you, redirect the questions to the group. This also encourages them to speak to each other. Don't echo the children's responses to questions, however. When you do this, it implies two things: that the answer has no validity unless you say it too, and that the child isn't responsible for speaking up loudly and clearly.

Don't be afraid of silence. Wait at least five seconds before jumping in to save the discussion. Learn to appreciate the difference between thoughtful silence and a lull in the discussion. End the discussion when energy is high; don't beat the topic to death.

The other kind of communication I would like to consider is the day-to-day communicating that goes on among students and between teachers and students. Is that communication as positive and supportive as it could be? This is an important question, and it relates to something I discussed at the beginning of the book. I believe that a positive and caring classroom community is the most conducive to creative conflict resolution. I also believe, and my teaching experience confirms, that there are fewer conflicts in a classroom where children are caring and respectful toward each other.

Sadly, many of our students must be taught how to be respectful, courteous, even just plain nice to each other. The activities that follow emphasize the benefits to the kids of behaving in this way. There is a payoff for being a nice guy or gal. When students realize this, you see a dramatic and very pleasant change in their behavior.

Put-downs

Grades K–6

Procedure:

1. Have the class brainstorm all of the mean, nasty words or phrases they've ever heard or said. Write all the contributions on the board. Ask, discussing the answers, "Where do we learn putdowns? How do they make people feel? Why do we say them? What would be the effect on the class if everyone always put everyone else down?"

2. Have the class relax by breathing slowly and deeply as you count to ten. Then conduct a guided fantasy by reading the list, pausing for a moment after each word or phrase and asking the class to think about what it would be like to be called that particular word.

3. Follow with the affirming statements lesson.

Affirming Statements

Grades K–6

Procedure:

1. Follow the put-downs activity with a brainstorming session on supportive things to say.

2. With young children, you may want to develop a class term for put-downs (e.g., grouch words, snarl words, rotten-apple words) and affirming statements (e.g., good-apple words, purr words).

3. A bulletin board on the theme of put-downs and affirming statements can be a very effective way to encourage positive change.

Discussion:

How would these affirming words and phrases make someone feel?

Why would they make them feel good?

What would be the effect on the class if we used these phrases more than put-downs?

Surprising Your Enemies

Grades K–6

Procedure:

Discuss enemies as suggested below. Have students think of an enemy they have and of some way they might pleasantly surprise that enemy. This needn't involve making up with the enemy, just doing something that will please him or her. Encourage volunteers to tell the class what they might do (without mentioning the enemy's name), and encourage them to do it.

Discussion:

How do you communicate with your enemies?

What are some of the communication patterns enemies get into with each other?

What would happen if you broke these patterns?

Why is it hard to take the first step in situations like this?

Respect and Community

Grades 2–6

Materials: three-by-five-inch index cards, pencils

Procedure:

1. With the class, define the words *respect* and *disrespect*. Emphasize that you needn't like someone to behave respectfully toward him or her.

2. Have the class think about how they would like to be treated, what they consider respectful behavior, and what a respectful classroom community would look like.

3. Distribute three-by-five cards and pencils. On the cards, have the kids describe things that would be said and done most often in their respectful classroom community. Post the cards on a bulletin board.

Discussion:

How would it feel to be in a respectful classroom community?

Is that a goal worth working toward?

How would we begin to work toward it?

Practicing Peaceable Behavior

Grades K–6

Procedure:

Have students volunteer for role play. Have them role-play both nasty and peaceable ways to say the following:

I don't want you to play.

I don't want your help.

You're not being fair.

You are making a mess.

You are bothering me.

Discussion:

Is it easier to be nasty or peaceable?

What makes being peaceable difficult?

Why might it be worth the effort?

Manners

Grades K–6

Procedure:

Manners, at their best, convey respect and promote smooth interactions. At their worst, they mask genuine feelings and create artificial, conflict-avoiding situations. Obviously, we should encourage manners at their best.

1. If your class doesn't regularly say "please," "thank you," and "excuse me," discuss their use and importance.

2. Do role plays with and without manners.

Discussion:

When would you use "please?" "Thank you?" "Excuse me?"

Why would you use them?

How do they show respect for others?

What are some aspects of courtesy other than saying "please" and "thank you?"

Why is courtesy important to the classroom community?

Class Caring Projects

Grades K–6

Procedure:

A class caring project can be just about anything that the class does as a whole to benefit other people—raising money for UNICEF, singing songs at an old-age home, putting on skits for younger children. This kind of project can be a wonderful way to promote a sense of community in the class while instilling in kids an awareness of how to put the abstract idea of caring into concrete action. Sometimes an idea for a project will arise spontaneously; more often you will have to get the ball rolling. Either way, class caring projects seem to follow these steps:

1. Choose a project.

2. Decide how to implement it.

3. Follow through.

It helps if the class initiates the idea, but more important is having the class figure out how to implement it, for instance, by deciding how to raise the money, by choosing the songs to sing, or by practicing the skits. It is also important that the class see tangible results such as thank-you notes from people in charge. Once a project is complete, get busy on another.

Caring Bulletin Board

Grades 1–3, (4–6)

Materials: tagboard

Procedure:

Ask students to become tattletales, telling you when they see acts of caring on the part of another. Then, on a five-by-eight-inch tag, write the relevant student's name and describe what he or she did. Post the card on the caring bulletin board for three to five days, and then give it to the child to keep.

● Older students usually find this activity immature, but sometimes they surprise you with their enthusiasm for it. This can also be a great schoolwide activity.

Caring Assignments

Grades 3–6

Procedure:

1. Older students are in a position to appreciate how difficult it can be to perform acts of caring in the real world. Discuss these difficulties and list them on the board.

2. Give caring assignments to students and have them report back. Some examples:

> Smile and say hello to five strangers on the street.

> Do something nice for someone you know dislikes you.

> Go to a supermarket and offer to carry an elderly person's groceries for free.

Once they get the idea, kids come up with great caring assignments.

Discussion:

> How did people react to your act of caring?

> Why do you think they were pleased or suspicious or hostile?

> How did their reaction influence you?

How did it make you feel?

How might you overcome suspicion or hostility in people?

Notes

1. David Shiman, *The Prejudice Book* (New York: Anti-Defamation League, 1979), pp. 26–27. Adapted with permission.

2. Adapted with permission of MacMillan Publishing Company from *Reality Games* by Saville Sax and Sandra Hollander. Copyright © 1972 by Saville Sax and Sandra Hollander.

3. Educators for Social Responsibility, *A Day of Dialogue: Planning and Curriculum Resource Guide* (Boston, 1982). Used with permission.

Chapter 6

Helping Students Handle Anger, Frustration, and Aggression

When I taught second grade, I would schedule late Tuesday and Thursday afternoons for various affective education activities. I didn't realize how much my students identified that as feelings time until the day I heard one child say to another, "You always try to make me feel bad. I'm going to tell." To this, the other child taunted, "He'll make you wait 'til Tuesday!"

Anyone who teaches knows that children do not leave their feelings outside the classroom door; each morning you face a room full of whole children. And all day, every day, they react to things emotionally. They don't wait until Tuesday at two. Particularly in conflict situations, they express emotions quickly and strongly.

When children do not know constructive ways to express anger and frustration, they frequently become aggressive, and aggressive behavior leads to conflict. Let's begin with aggression then, and work from there.

The Nature of Aggression

Aggression is not an emotion; it is an expression of emotion. It is defined as any behavior intended to harm another person, either physically or emotionally. Intent to harm is the crucial factor. A dentist causes you pain, but she or he doesn't mean to harm you. Similarly, a student may harm another accidentally, but the absence of intent to harm keeps the action from being aggressive. (Incidentally, the use of the term *aggressive* as denoting a positive trait is generally being replaced by the use of the more appropriate term *assertive*.)

Aggression usually occurs as a result of an excited emotional state. Anger and frustration are the emotions that frequently lead to aggression, although (oddly enough) even positive emotional excitement can lead to aggression. Once a child is excited, some incident or action is perceived as threatening to the child's resources, needs, or values. This triggers aggressive behavior in response to the perceived threat.

Much of what is popularly believed about aggression comes from the writings of Sigmund Freud and Konrad Lorenz, both of whom hold that aggression is an inborn trait, and that its expression—in harmless ways—is essential to human health. The problem with these theories is that they don't hold up under most subsequent research. It now seems clear that, although the capacity for violence is certainly inborn, its expression depends on many factors, the first and foremost being what has been learned.[1] Aggression seems to be learned primarily through example, reward, and the perception of aggressors as successful people.

In Albert Bandura's famous studies, children were shown models who behaved aggressively and nonaggressively toward a four-foot inflatable doll named Bobo. In various versions of the experiment, aggression and nonaggression toward the Bobo doll were modeled in animations and by actors on film and TV; children viewed the results. If the children saw aggression, they always imitated it. Studies by other researchers have confirmed that what children learn from such modeling has lasting effects on their behavior. Studies have also been conducted concerning the effects of TV violence on children's aggression. The depressing conclusion is the same.[2]

Modeling not only shows how to be aggressive; it implies that being aggressive is all right. There are countless rewards for aggression, particularly in a society as competitive as ours. Often unwittingly, we model aggression and reward it as the way to win, to get what you want. And winning, as any child will tell you, is important.

There are, of course, ways to get what one wants without being aggressive. And the positive side to all this is that just as children learn aggressive behavior, so can they learn peaceable behavior.

Emotional Expression and Self-control

Most people would agree that emotions should be expressed, not suppressed or bottled up. For this reason, many people are uncomfortable with the concept of teaching emotional control to children. They equate it with the suppression of emotions and see it as ultimately producing tense, miserable adults. Self-control, they seem to feel, is something children simply acquire in the process of growing up. The fact is that emotional expression of any sort is learned, be it aggressive or peaceable. So is self-control. By teaching children positive ways to express their emotions, we can improve the way they handle their conflicts.

While we're at it, there is another important distinction to make. Just as there is a difference between controlling emotions and suppressing emotions, so is there a difference between expressing emotions and venting them, or letting off steam. The idea that anger, frustration, and aggression can be vented is a popular one, a holdover from the theories of Freud and Lorenz. In saying that aggression is inborn, their logical conclusion was that if it was not released or displaced—vented, as it were—the aggressive feelings would build up and have dire effects on a person's physical and emotional health. As it happens, there is virtually no scientific support for this theory. People are not pressure cookers. In fact, the evidence indicates that venting aggressive feelings by hitting a punching bag or kicking a doll or any of a number of other violent releases only makes you feel more hostile and aggressive. The cliché is true: violence begets violence.

Research indicates that the most effective method for releasing angry and aggressive feelings is either to express them directly to the one who is responsible for them or to cool off and let the hostility dissipate. Being distracted or amused to the point of laughter are two of the best ways to cool off, by the way.

As professionals, it is particularly important that our emotions enhance, not interfere with, our dealings with students. Sometimes, in order to deal fairly with a child, we must detach ourselves from the anger, frustration, and aggression the child evokes from us. If you find yourself carrying around angry, hostile feelings toward a child, the following exercise can help you to let go of some of these feelings. It can especially help you deal with students who are consistently and thoroughly aggravating.

Exercise

The following guided fantasy can help you relax and clear your mind of hostility. Sit in a comfortable position. Relax your muscles and begin breathing deeply and slowly. Count to ten, inhaling on one, exhaling on two, inhaling on three, and so on. When you reach ten, count back down to one.

Imagine yourself in a room facing the child who angers you so. She or he is in a chair; you are standing. She or he cannot react in any way to you. Imagine yourself gently tossing eggs at the child. As you throw each egg, imagine yourself saying what each egg represents: "This one is for swearing at me in class; this one is for throwing the erasers out the windows; this one is for . . . ." Throw an egg for everything that ever angered or frustrated you about this child.

Now imagine the child sitting there covered with eggs. She or he looks ridiculous. Imagine yourself laughing. As you laugh, each egg turns into a balloon and begins to rise. Watch "swearing at me in class" float away. Watch "dropping your paint brush down the drain" float away. Watch all the things that made you angry or frustrated drift quietly away from you forever. And now watch the child begin to float away, too. Higher and higher. For this moment, he or she is out of your life, and you are left sitting in an idyllic garden.

Approaching Emotions as a Subject

Children often question whether emotions are a legitimate topic for discussion in school. They tend to show discomfort at the mention of emotional issues. There is no doubt that affective education can be conducted inappropriately; on the other hand, it's naive to think that you can teach anything without dealing with the emotional aspect. For these somewhat conflicting reasons, I advocate a straightforward approach to emotions in the classroom.

First, work on feelings as a topic throughout the day. This will discourage the Tuesday-at-two attitude I described earlier. Casually refer to the affective aspects of the children's day-to-day business in the classroom: "I feel good because you're working hard today." "I'm disappointed in the story we just read. Did you like it?" Such messages point out the affective component of daily life and establish emotions as a legitimate classroom topic.

Let the kids know how you feel at different times of the day. If you're feeling grouchy, say so; they'll appreciate the warning.

When you conduct activities such as sharing circles (discussed later in this chapter), remember that you are not conducting group therapy. Be respectful of students' privacy. When you do have sharing circles, share of yourself as well. This reinforces the legitimacy of emotional expression and sets a standard for what is acceptable to share. Being very matter-of-fact about the things you discuss helps your students feel more comfortable.

Keep an eye on how you express your own emotions in the classroom. Do you express them honestly? Do you express them appropriately? Is your behavior really what you want to model?

Make positive emotional expression a part of your unique classroom community's way of doing things. Develop key phrases with your class to remind them of ways to control their emotions. For example, I had one class which loved the Happy Valley exercise discussed later in this chapter. Whenever anyone got angry, the class would chorus, "Time to visit Happy Valley!" It sounded as if they were demented, but it worked. I also had a kindergarten class that was absolutely smitten with the draining and ballooning activities discussed below. They would drain and balloon at the drop of a hat, until I finally had to sit a few of them down and explain that it was not always appropriate to drain or balloon.

Described below are activities that focus on three areas of positive emotional expression that are most relevant to conflict and conflict resolution:

identifying emotions and their sources

learning positive ways to express emotions

learning self-control

Identifying Emotions

These activities are designed to help children increase their emotion-related vocabularies; better understand the sources of feelings; and, perhaps most importantly, identify how other people are feeling.

Because this area is so well covered in other sources, only a few activities are included. These are mostly short and simple ones that can be easily integrated in the course of the day.

React

Grades 1–4

Materials: fifteen to twenty cards with one emotion noted on each

Procedure:

This activity is a good change of pace, a way to get the kids up and moving after they've been sitting for a while.

1. Have a student draw a card and read the emotion listed. The other children should react with their faces and bodies to the feeling.

2. Alternatively, have a student draw a card and, without showing the class, react. The class tries to guess the emotion noted on the card.

Discussion:

What does body language say about how a person feels?

Can people say one thing with their bodies and another with their words?

How would body language be used in conflicts?

Feelings Dictionary

Grades K, 1, (2, 3)

Materials: magazines, paper, pencil or marker

Procedure:

1. Label sheets of paper with the names of different emotions. Have the children look through magazines for pictures that illustrate the feelings.

2. Older children can brainstorm associations the feelings evoke. They can also look for more subtle shades of difference in emotions.

Discussion:

What makes people feel ——?

Have you ever felt that way?

What did you do about the feeling?

The Happy-Sad-Mad Way

Grades K–3

Procedure:

1. Focus on one emotion (for instance, anger) each time you do this activity. Have the children perform different actions in a way that reflects that emotion. (For instance, have them walk, smile, shake hands, and sweep the floor, all angrily.)

2. Once they have the idea, have them suggest actions to pantomime in a feeling way.

Discussion:

How do people let you know what they're feeling without expressing it in words?

What clues could you watch for?

What things make you feel ——?

Ergo

Grades 3–6

Materials: pencils, paper

Procedure:

1. Explain that *ergo* means *therefore* in Latin.

2. Have students write endings for the following incomplete statements:

Bill pushed Jane; ergo . . .

Paul laughed; ergo . . .

Mary's face turned red; ergo . . .

Danny was crying; ergo . . .

Leroy is staring out the window; ergo . . .

3. Have students share their ergo responses and discuss.

Discussion:

What clues did you use to figure out your ergos?

In what ways did you draw on your own experience?

What other kinds of information would be useful in figuring out the ergos?

How could you find that information?

Feeling Vocabularies

Grades (K–2), 3–6

Procedure:

1. Explain to the class that using a broad vocabulary of feeling words will make their writing more interesting. Have them brainstorm a list of every emotion-related word they've ever heard.

2. Have volunteers give examples of situations that might elicit these emotions.

Discussion:

What is the difference between —— and ——?

What causes you to feel ——?

How would any of these words be useful in your writing?

🍎 Do this with younger children as a purely affective exercise, unrelated to language arts.

Manipulated Emotions

Grades K-3, (4-6)

Procedure:

Have students find examples of sounds or music that evoke emotion. Then have them find visual images that do the same.

🍎 With older students, use this activity as a springboard for discussion of how emotions are manipulated by media. Discuss why this is useful to some people (such as advertisers) and why it is beneficial for students to be aware of it. Have students keep a log for one week, recording when and how their emotions are manipulated.

Discussion:

When you [hear these sounds, see these images] how does that make you feel?

How can you tell if someone is trying to manipulate your emotions?

Why would someone want to do that?

Enemies

Grades (K-2), 3-6

Materials: *Let's Be Enemies* by Janice May Udry, three-by-five-inch index cards, pencils

Procedure:

1. Introduce this activity to older kids by saying, "You may remember this book." Read the book *Let's Be Enemies* out loud. Brainstorm: "What are the things we commonly say about enemies? Why do we say them?"

2. Distribute three-by-five cards. Have the kids describe an advantage of having an enemy on one side, and a disadvantage of having an enemy on the other. Have them read their notes to the rest of the class, and discuss.

Discussion:

Do little kids understand what an enemy is?

What did you think an enemy was when you were little?

Do you have enemies now?

How might you convert an enemy to a friend?

Why are there countries that used to be our enemies that are now our friends?

What Is Hate?

Grades (K, 1), 2–6

Materials: paper, pencils, crayons

Procedure:

1. Ask the class to draw pictures of hate. Don't give any more direction than this, and see what the kids come up with. Discuss the results.

2. Have students complete the sentence stub "Hate is . . ." five times. Have them include mention of causes of hate and the behavior it inspires.

3. Have students write about an experience they had hating someone or something and how they overcame the hate.

Discussion:

Are there degrees of hate?

What is the opposite of hate?

What kinds of things does hate cause people to do?

Can hate change? How?

How is hate related to anger? Can you hate and not be angry?

🍎 With younger children, stop after the drawing exercise, and use the pictures as a springboard for discussion.

Feeling Definitions

Grades 2–4

Materials: pencils, paper

Procedure:

1. Focus on one emotion each time you do this activity. Have the children write about emotions in this format:

    To feel —— means ——.

    What makes me feel —— is ——.

    I know other people feel —— when ——.

2. Have volunteers read their answers, and discuss them.

Discussion:

How did you respond to the statements?

Which aspects were the most difficult to answer?

How do you know someone feels ——?

Sharing Circles

Grades K–6

Procedure:

A sharing circle is a type of classroom meeting. Its purpose is to encourage children to share feelings and opinions about different issues, or to examine emotions and how they relate to daily life. The suggestions in chapter three on classroom meetings and in chapter five on classroom discussions also apply here.

One good technique to use in sharing circles is to have students complete sentence stubs, such as:

A time I was happy was . . .

Something that makes me frightened . . .

When I'm angry, . . .

It's obvious from these examples that you must be sensitive to your students and how much or little they prefer to share in a circle. You should explain your reason for using a particular sentence stub. You should also tell students that they have the right to pass, a right they may use excessively at first. There is nothing to be gained by forcing students to participate in this kind of activity. There's a big difference between drawing students out and badgering them into participating.

Trust is crucial to the success of sharing circles. You must assess the level of trust in your classroom yourself. The next activity can help you determine the limits of your sharing circles.

Privacy Lists

Grades 2–6

Materials: writing paper, pencils, three large sheets of paper, markers, tape

Procedure:

1. Have each student list three or four things that would be easy to talk about with the class, then three things that would be difficult to discuss, and finally three things he or she would not share. Students should not put their names on papers.

2. Collect the papers. Label the large sheets of paper *Easy, Difficult,* and *Private*; tape them to the board; and list on them the major topics the students wrote. Do not transcribe anything that might be linked to a particular student.

3. Assure students that you have no intention of invading their privacy in any activity.

Discussion:

What makes some things easy to talk about?

Why are others more difficult?

Why is it important not to force people to talk about private things?

What are some ways you could let others know when discussions are getting too personal?

Why is trust important to our classroom community?

Learning Positive Ways to Express Emotions

The emphasis in these lessons is clearly on what could be called negative emotions (anger and frustration) because these are the most relevant to conflict. It's important to reward positive expressions of these emotions when you see them. Students often have at their command, without really knowing it, a fund of positive ways to express negative emotions. The concept that anger might be responsibly and constructively used may be a revelation to them.

The connection between these activities and conflict may not be immediately obvious to the students. Emphasize the relationship whenever you can.

Aggression

Grades K–4, (5, 6)

Procedure:

1. Write the word *aggression* on the board and explain that it means an attempt to hurt others physically or emotionally.

2. Ask, "Have you ever behaved aggressively? What made you feel that you wanted to hurt someone?" Explain, "In conflict situations, people sometimes behave aggressively because they are angry or frustrated. Over the next few weeks, we'll be looking at ways to express emotions nonaggressively."

Discussion:

Why do people behave aggressively?

What are the results of behaving aggressively?

Does being aggressive help you get what you want?

What makes you behave aggressively?

🍎 With older children, you can look at aggressive behavior in the community and the world. "Are people innately aggressive?" is an interesting question for them to research. "What are socially acceptable and unacceptable ways to express aggression?" is another.

Grump and Growl[3]

Grades K–6

Procedure:

I schedule grump and growl sessions weekly, more often if necessary. The class sits in a circle, and everyone gets a chance to say what angered, annoyed, or frustrated him or her that week. Each student can say who was involved, what was done about the problem, and whether or not the situation was cleared up to the student's satisfaction. Unresolved problems can be turned over to the group for a problem-solving session.

🍎 With young children, some little gimmick such as an anger puppet or a magic microphone (a wooden dowel with two feet of yarn attached) adds fun to this activity.

The Bug Board

Grades K–3

Materials: crayons, drawing paper

Procedure:

1. Discuss feeling bugged, i.e., annoyed or angry.

2. Have the children draw and label a picture of something that bugs them. Young children will probably have to dictate labels to you.

3. Have the children show their pictures to each other and discuss them. Then post them on a bulletin board. This becomes the bug board. Use the situations pictured as situations for the problem puppets to explore.

Discussion:

What do you do when someone or something bugs you?

What else could you do?

Do two or more of you get bugged by the same thing?

Bug Line

Grades 3–6

Materials: pencils, paper

Procedure:

This is a more sophisticated version of the previous activity.

1. Have students list ten things that bug them. Then have them rank order the list from mildly annoying to really infuriating, one to ten.

2. Have volunteers share all the level one items, then all the level five items, and finally all the level ten items.

Discussion:

How do you let people know that they are bugging you?

How do you get them to stop?

What do you do that bugs others?

How would you like them to tell you to stop?

The Anger List

Grades (K, 1), 2–6

Procedure:

1. Brainstorm an anger list with the class. This should be a list of all the ways they can think of to express anger.

2. Discuss the list and decide which modes of expression are likely to be dangerous or hurtful (aggressive), and draw a line through them. Explain that the line simply means *not recommended.*

3. Describe to the class a situation that would be likely to provoke anger. Have the entire class choose and then pantomime a response from the anger list. Repeat for several different anger list responses.

Discussion:

Which of these might hurt someone or be dangerous in some way?

Which might get you into trouble?

Have you had an experience with one of the recommended ones that you could share?

Anger Interviews

Grades 2–6

Procedure:

1. With the class, develop a questionnaire about anger, including such items as "What makes you angry?" and "What do you do when you're angry?"

2. Have students interview family and friends and then share the results with the class.

Discussion:

What were some especially good ways to express anger?

How did people react to your questions?

Anger Bubbles

Grades 2–6

Procedure:

1. Put the picture series shown here on the chalkboard or a bulletin board.

1. *Why am I angry?*

2. *At whom am I angry?*

3. *How angry am I on a scale of one to ten?*

4. *What am I going to do about it?*

2. Tell students that, when they are angry, they should try imagining themselves as comic book characters with these thought bubbles. Suggest that they learn to answer these questions before acting.

Discussion:

Why might answering these questions help you express anger effectively?

Why might it help to rank your anger on a scale of one to ten?

What are some of the ways you might express it?

What can you do if you're not angry at any particular person?

Anger Fantasy

Grades K–6

Procedure:

1. Have the students sit comfortably with eyes closed. As you count to ten, they should take a deep breath for each count. When you reach ten, count backward to one as the students continue deep breathing.

2. Say, pausing at appropriate points, "In this guided fantasy you will be thinking about anger. Think of someone in the class who has made you angry. Think of what she or he did. Imagine the details clearly. Why did it make you angry? Think of an aggressive response to that person. Imagine how the person would react to that. Now think of a positive way to express your anger. Make sure the person knows you are angry. How might she or he respond? Now think of three things you like about that person, even if they are small things."

Discussion:

What kind of aggressive response did you think of making?

How did you think the person would react?

What kind of positive response did you think of making?

How would she or he respond?

Why did I ask you to think of three things you liked about that person?

Finding the Positive[4]

Grades K–6

Procedure:

1. Explain that often, even though we may feel angry or aggressive or frustrated, we also have positive feelings.

2. Ask for volunteers to describe situations that evoked negative emotions. Make a chart on the board using the following format:

negative feeling	situation	positive feeling
cheated	playing Monopoly with classmates	proud of being honest
insulted	being called names on the playground	grown-up—didn't call names back
annoyed	playing ball with inept players	grown-up—didn't get mad; enjoyed game for what it was worth

Discussion:

Why is it hard to think of positive things?

Why would it be helpful to think of positive things?

Using Anger Constructively

Grades 5, 6

Procedure:

Like conflict, anger can have constructive results for society. It has motivated social change and growth.

1. Have each student research one of the following people and report on what injustice angered them and the type of social action they were inspired to take. Other interesting questions concern what conflicts they encountered and how they responded.

Martin Luther King, Jr.	Jane Addams
Susan B. Anthony	Ralph Nader
Lucretia Mott	Rachel Carson
Dorothy Dix	Joan Baez
Ida Tarbell	Gloria Steinem
Mohandas K. Gandhi	Emma Goldman

2. Have students locate newspaper accounts of people who are using their anger constructively and destructively.

Discussion:

What did you learn from this activity?

How might you use anger constructively?

What is an issue in society that makes you angry?

Respect and Reservations

Grades 4–6

Procedure:

1. Discuss ways to get people to stop doing annoying things. Suggest that one way to do this is to talk about R&R—respect and reservations. First you say something that you respect and appreciate about that person, and then you say what it is you have reservations about. Suggest the following format: "I like it when you ——, but I have reservations about the way you ——."
2. Give students opportunities to practice through such devices as role plays, skits, and comic strip assignments.

Discussion:

Why is it easier to hear criticism when it comes with appreciation?

Why might it be good for the critic to remember something good about the other person?

In what kinds of situations might it be appropriate to use this technique?

When might it be inappropriate?

Pennies[5]

Grades 3–6	**Materials:** fifteen pennies per child

Procedure:

1. Give each student fifteen pennies. Tell them that their task is to set the pennies in a row on end. This is difficult but not impossible.

2. As the students work, watch for different reactions to the frustration: some students will get angry, some will withdraw, some will give up, and so on. (Mention the reactions later, during discussion.)

3. After ten minutes or so (when students are beginning to get very frustrated), end the activity, and discuss it.

Discussion:

What did you think when you first heard the activity described?

What did you think when you first tried to do it?

After you had tried and failed for a while, how did you feel?

Would it have been a less frustrating experience if you had been working with other people?

What other kinds of situations frustrate you?

What can you do in frustrating situations?

🍎 Leave some pennies in a jar for students to fool with during free time. There's always someone who wants to keep trying until it works.

House of Cards

Grades 2–6	**Materials:** a deck of cards for every three students

Procedure:

1. Divide the students into groups of three. Give each group a deck of cards, and instruct them to build a three-storied house using only the cards.

2. As with the pennies activity, watch for signs of frustration. Note how frustration is expressed among group members.

3. After ten minutes or so (when students are beginning to get very frustrated), end the activity, and discuss it.

Discussion:

What did you think when you first heard the activity described?

What did you think when you first tried to do it?

After you had tried and failed for a while, how did you feel?

How did you express frustration to group members?

Could you feel yourself getting angry?

Were conflicts beginning to arise?

What other kinds of situations frustrate you?

What can you do in frustrating situations?

Happy Valley

Grades 2-6

Procedure:
Teach students to take a trip to Happy Valley. Use this guided fantasy several times; then suggest they use it on their own when particularly excited. Say, "Imagine you are walking through a tunnel. It's dark. Suddenly the walls of the tunnel catch fire. You're safe, but the walls are burning. Then you reach the end of the tunnel and find a tiny door. Bend over, and open the door. Walk through. The fire and dark are behind you now; you're walking down steps into Happy Valley. Happy Valley is beautiful and filled with things you like to do. See, something you've always wanted to do is waiting to be done over there on the right. Imagine yourself doing that activity. There's a river on the right. In the river is an island, and on the island are the people you are mad at. Wave to them. They can't get near you now; they can't hurt you or make you mad now. They can't get near Happy Valley. Turn your back on them and enjoy Happy Valley some more. When you're ready, leave Happy Valley, refreshed and calm, and not angry and frustrated any more.''

Draining

Grades K-6

Procedure:

1. Have the children tense all their muscles and breathe in. Then they should hold their muscles and breathe for five seconds. Starting with the head, they should then relax down to the feet, exhaling as they do. Repeat several times.

2. Once they have the knack, have them think of someone at whom they are angry or something that has frustrated them. Have them tense up, thinking of the anger or frustration. Then, as they relax, tell them that the anger is draining out of them. All that emotion is leaking out the tips of their toes and is now in a puddle at their feet.

3. Once they have drained, they should stand aside, out of the puddle, and leave the anger behind.

🍎 Seemingly ridiculous, this is a remarkably effective technique for adult or child. Try it!

Discussion:
When might you drain?

How might it help you feel?

Why would it be a good thing to step aside from anger or frustration?

Ballooning

Grades K-3

Procedure:

1. Explain that one way to cool off when you are angry is to take deep breaths. Ballooning is one way to do this.

2. Have the children fill their lungs with air and raise their arms as if

they were balloons. Next, have them slowly release the air and shrivel up like deflated balloons. Repeat three times in all.

Discussion:

How do you feel after ballooning three times?

Do you think it would help you calm down if you were angry?

When might you want to try ballooning?

Distracting

Grades K–4

Procedure:

1. Establish a laughing corner. Laughter can dissipate anger and aggression. Have a scrapbook of cartoons and books of jokes there. You might also have clay, paints, little toys, balloons—whatever an angry child might use to distract himself or herself.

2. List the steps for a distraction dance. Post the following sequence to be completed quickly:

    Clap three times.

    Sit on the floor.

    Kick your right foot.

    Kick your left foot.

    Jump up.

    Wave arms.

    Breathe in—fill up with air.

    Deflate slowly, like a balloon, onto the floor.

    In slow motion, stand.

    Turn around three times.

    Say aloud, "I'm calm now."

Learning Self-control

Self-control isn't learned overnight. Neither is it accomplished by accident. These activities aim to give students an understanding of the process involved in self-control. They begin by examining their own personal power, first over others and then over themselves. The reason for this emphasis on power is that children are often not aware of their power, and yet self-control is largely a conscious exercise of power over self. Once they have this awareness of their own power, they are ready to understand the link between emotions and behavior and, finally, to develop a personal conduct code. Meanwhile, they practice ways to make their needs and desires known without resorting to aggression.

Bossy, Bossy

Grades K–3

Materials: list of tasks (see below)

Procedure:

Give several different children opportunities to be the boss. The boss is allowed to give someone any of the instructions on the list below.

Jump up and down three times.

Recite "Mary Had a Little Lamb."

Walk around your desk.

Say "Howdy!" to ——.

Flap like a bird.

Say your name three times.

Shake hands with ——.

Rub your stomach and pat your head at the same time.

Discussion:

How did it feel to be the boss?

How did it feel to be bossed?

What if you were bossed all the time?

Could the boss have made people mad at him or her? How?

What would have happened if someone had refused to be bossed?

Kid Power

Grades 2–6

Materials: pencils, paper

Procedure:

1. Have each student list three ways he or she can make the teacher happy and three ways he or she can make the teacher unhappy. Repeat for parents and friends.

2. Have them each list three ways to make themselves happy without making anyone else unhappy.

Discussion:

What were some of the ways to make people happy? Unhappy?

Do you do these things?

When might you want to make someone happy?

When might you want to make someone unhappy?

What is power?

What power do people have over you?

What power do you have over other people?

What power do you have over yourself?

Want To, Have To

Grades 3–6

Materials: pencils, paper

Procedure:

1. Have each child write about five things she or he has to do at home or school, in the following format: "I have to ——."

2. Have them rewrite the sentences, saying, instead, "I choose to ——." Identify which of the five are still "have to" things.

3. List some of the controls imposed by friends, family, school, community, and media.

4. List some inner controls, i.e., controls that are self-imposed.

Discussion:

Which "choose to" sentences still involved "have to" things?

Why were they "have to"—what controls were involved?

What would happen if you didn't do them?

Do you really have to, or are you choosing not to face negative consequences?

What are the differences between outer (external) and inner (internal) controls?

How do they affect your behavior?

Positive Controls

Grades 3–6

Procedure:

1. Ask, "What would happen if there were no controls on people's anger, frustration, or aggression? What behavior would result? What would life be like?"

2. With the class, brainstorm a list of the consequences of uncontrolled emotions, both for the individual and for society.

3. Or use the theme as a topic for a writing exercise: have the students describe a society where people have no controls, internal or external, on their behavior.

Discussion:

Of what use are controls?

Can there be too many controls? What might happen if there were too many controls?

Would you rather have controls come from outside you or inside you?

Responding to Aggressive Behavior

Grades 3–6

Materials: worksheet on responding to aggressive behavior (see Appendix)

Procedure:

Distribute the worksheet. Discuss the meaning of *short-term* and *long-range*. Discuss the first situation described on the worksheet with the class; then have them complete it independently. Discuss.

● As an alternative, do not reproduce the worksheet, but simply use the descriptions of situations as discussion starters.

Discussion:

Which was easier to predict, long-range or short-term effects?

Why is it helpful to look at both?

What problems do you encounter in confronting aggressive behavior?

Personal Conduct Code

Grades 4–6

Materials: pencils, paper

Procedure:

Have students write down three endings to the following incomplete sentences:

In frustrating situations, I will try to . . .

When I feel angry and aggressive, I will try to . . .

When I am in a conflict situation, I will try to . . .

Discussion:

What did you decide to write?

How did you come to those decisions?

What does it mean to develop a personal code of conduct?

What kind of commitment are you making?

Will it be easy or hard to keep to the code?

How could you help each other stick to your codes?

Notes

1. For an excellent and highly readable summary of current research on aggression and its relationship to conflict, see Ronald Baily, *Violence and Aggression* (New York: Time-Life, 1976).

2. See Albert Bandura, *Aggression, A Social Learning Analysis* (Englewood Cliffs, N.J.: Prentice-Hall, 1973).

3. I learned this technique from Kathy Allen.

4. Stanley A. Fagen et al., *Teaching Children Self-Control: Preventing Emotional and Learning Problems in the Elementary School* (Columbus, Ohio: Chas. Merrill, 1975), p. 176. Adapted with permission.

5. I learned this activity from Bill Graf.

Chapter 7

Teaching Cooperation

... the society of man has survived
because the cooperation of its members
has made survival possible.
—Ashley Montague

Every year I ask my students what it means to cooperate. Usually they answer something like, "It means do what you tell us." This year someone said, "It means, don't be always giving you a hard time!" Cooperation is a word we teachers use frequently. We assume that students know what cooperation is, and we assume that they know how to cooperate. Neither of these assumptions is necessarily valid.

To cooperate is to work together toward mutual goals. In this chapter, we will be discussing cooperation primarily as it relates to working in groups, but it is important to keep in mind that groups are not necessary to cooperation. Cooperation may involve working together in one room; it may involve working at opposite ends of the school. Scientists from different countries often cooperate without ever seeing each other or even speaking the same language.

Of all the aspects of the peaceable classroom, cooperation is in many ways the most important. Creative conflict resolution, tolerant attitudes, good communication habits, and appropriate sharing of feelings are far more likely when children know how to work together. Cooperation also engenders a sense of community and good feeling.

Cooperation and Competition

Before we discuss cooperation further, we need to look at its opposite—competition. American classrooms are generally conceded to be highly competitive places. Our grouping and grading practices are competitive; even many of our teaching strategies are competitive. And competitive situations are very likely to produce conflict.

Now, this is not necessarily bad. Conflict, as I said in chapter one, is necessary for growth. And, as our culture is certainly based on competition, we generally believe that students need to learn to compete to get along in what we call real life. For conflict to lead to growth, however, it must be responded to creatively, in a win-win fashion. Competition by its very nature mandates a win-lose outcome. As for the notion of preparing students for life, consider the following.

Psychologists Linden Nelson, Spencer Kagen, and Millard Madsen conducted a series of experiments to assess children's cooperative ability. Most of the tasks required children to cooperate to earn prizes. The research subjects were children from the United States and Mexico, aged five to ten, from both rural and urban backgrounds. In almost all instances, the Anglo-American children ranked low in both their ability to cooperate and their willingness to do so. Older children were, in fact, so conditioned to think competitively that they could not think cooperatively even when it was in their best interests to do so.

But there was more than a simple lack of cooperation skills. After observing an experiment where children were given the choice of taking or not taking toys from their opponents, Nelson and Kagen concluded, "Anglo-American children are not only irrationally competitive, they are almost sadistically rivalrous. Given a choice, Anglo-American children took toys away from the peers on 78 per cent of the trials even when they could not keep the toys for themselves. Observing the success of their actions, some of the children gloated, 'Ha! Ha! Now you won't get a toy.'"[1]

Can that be called preparing students for life?

Competition is so thoroughly interwoven with American culture and the American way of life that a number of myths have become solidly entrenched in our thinking.[2] Try the following quiz. You might be surprised.

Exercise

Decide if you think each statement is true or false.

1. Competition builds character.

2. Cooperation gives lazy students a free ride on the backs of the hard workers.

3. Competition builds confidence and self-esteem.

4. In cooperative situations, students never have to challenge themselves.

5. Students need to learn to compete in a competitive society.

6. Competition is sometimes appropriate in a school setting.

7. Competition builds a healthy desire to avoid failure.

8. Kids would rather be in cooperative settings.

9. Cooperation forces conformity to the group.

10. Cooperation often leads to greater achievement than competition.

Compare your answers with the correct ones:

1. False. No evidence exists to support the claim that competition builds character. However, there is evidence to the contrary, such as that presented by Nelson and Kagen, as discussed above.

2. False. Research suggests that students work harder in groups. My own experience certainly confirms this. It depends, in part, on how students learn to work in groups. Students can be taught not to allow freeloading.

3. False. Competition builds confidence only if you win; in a competitive situation, most people can't win. In addition, the pressure is on the winner to keep winning.

4. False. Students are more likely to take risks and extend themselves in a cooperative and supportive group than in a competitive situation that penalizes losing.

5. True. Children do need to learn how to compete, but it is virtually impossible to grow up in this country without learning how to compete. On the other hand, the vast majority of human interaction is cooperative. Competition is, in reality, a very small part of our interaction.

6. True. There are a few situations in which competition enhances learning, particularly rote learning.

7. True. Competition probably does lead to a desire to avoid failure. The question is whether failure is so terrible. Failure is an important part of learning, but competitive situations equate it with losing. Thomas Edison had to make five hundred tries before he succeeded in inventing the electric light. In other words, he "lost" five hundred times.

8. True. Given a choice, students will most likely choose a cooperative learning situation, particularly if they have been in one.

9. False. The only conformity required in a cooperative situation is the mutuality of goals. How the group reaches the goals and the contributions each person makes are up to individuals in the group. Whether or not conformity becomes a problem depends on how you teach children to work in groups.

10. True. Neither competition nor cooperation guarantees striving for excellence, but cooperation is more likely to elicit this.

Fostering Cooperation

There are three steps involved in reducing competition and encouraging cooperation:

1. Change classroom practices and build a sense of community.

2. Train the children in the skill of cooperation.

3. Use cooperative learning strategies.

There are two advantages for you when you teach cooperation. One is that academic performance often increases when cooperative activities are appropriately used. The other advantage is one I noticed right away when I first began to use cooperative games and activities in my own classroom: namely, there were measurably fewer conflicts in my classroom and more willingness to look for creative, win-win resolutions to the conflicts that did occur.

Changing classroom practices means simply establishing routines and procedures that encourage and reward cooperation. In the People's Republic of China, the children's clothing often buttons down the back. Thus, children must help each other dress and undress. Although some of us Americans are uncomfortable with that example, the point is worth heeding: if you want kids to help each other, give them opportunities to do so.

For example, when I taught kindergarten, untied shoes were one of the banes of my existence. (Snowsuits were the other.) I hated tying shoes. Finally, it occurred to me to have those children who could tie shoes do the tying. Not only were they more patient about it than I; they enjoyed it more.

For another example, every teacher has experienced the frustration of facing a class filled with raised hands or a line of children at his or her desk, all of whom have one question or another. Why can't they help each other out? If you are concerned that they will simply give each other the answers—a legitimate concern—then teach them that helping is different from simply giving out answers. Explain that helping is explaining the directions, assisting someone in sounding out a puzzling word, and so on. Giving the answers isn't really helping anyone. (One teacher I know has made it a rule that students cannot ask her for help until they've asked everyone in their group of four.)

Taking this one step further, many teachers have had great success with peer tutoring programs. Many children learn better from other children than from adults. Peer tutors don't need to be the best at a particular subject. If a child understands long division, then he or she can usually teach long division. Give the tutors some training in effective teaching techniques, emphasizing again that giving out answers is not teaching; and soon you will have a class full of assistants. Then, when a child comes to you needing help with vocabulary words or with using the dictionary or with practicing multiplication facts, you can ask that a tutor volunteer for this specific task. (Not all tutors can teach a particular subject, of course, and some tutor-tutee combinations are bad ones. Use your judgment.)

Teachers often ask me, "Won't the kids become turned off to cooperation if I make too much of it?" That depends on what is considered too much. You don't need to harp on it, but neither should you be afraid to label cooperative behavior when it occurs. After all, we don't hesitate to tell a student that he or she did something "all by yourself." There are plenty of opportunities in classrooms to say, "We did it together," or, "You did a good job cooperating." Don't let these opportunities go by.

The most basic way to encourage a feeling of community in a classroom is to develop projects to which the whole class can contribute. There's nothing new about this idea. The projects can be the old standards you did when you were in elementary school. They can be as simple as painting a class mural or baking cookies, or as involved as putting on a play or publishing a newspaper. These sorts of projects can be the focus of children's fondest memories of your classroom. Approach them with enthusiasm and watch carefully to see that everyone feels in some way included and important to the project.

The descriptions of activities in this chapter are grouped under the following headings:

Cooperative Games

Cooperation Activities

Cooperative Learning

Cooperative Games

A good way to build community and give kids a relaxed, informal chance to practice cooperation skills is through cooperative games. In the past few years, cooperative games have come into their own. All kinds of people have discovered that games don't necessarily involve competing and that people can play together rather than against each other.

Cooperative games are great fun and, as games, need no other justification. They are, however, also a splendid way to teach cooperation skills. Three things can be said of a good cooperative game:

1. Everyone wins. No one is singled out as the loser.

2. No one sits on the sidelines. Everyone gets to play.

3. The group is challenged to work together.

Cooperative games needn't necessarily replace competitive games (although I no longer have my students play any competitive games). Children can enjoy cooperative games and still play baseball, soccer, and so on. I look at cooperative games as a way of giving the other side—cooperation—equal time.

Form a Line

Grades K–6

Procedure:

1. This is a very basic cooperative activity. Start by having the class (or groups of five to ten) form a line. Then, without talking, have them make the shortest line they can; then, the longest.

2. Continue by having the students arrange themselves in a line from shortest to tallest. Again, they should do all this without talking.

3. More challenging variations exist: a line in order of birthdays, or oldest to youngest, or smallest feet to largest—all without talking.

Discussion:

Which were the easiest tasks? Most difficult? Why?

What problems did you encounter?

How did the no-talking rule affect the way you worked in groups?

How would being allowed to talk have changed things?

Bridges[3]

Grades K–6

Procedure:

1. Have partners of approximately equal size stand facing each other about six inches apart. Hands should be raised to shoulder level, with palms facing the partner's palms.

2. The players simultaneously fall forward, catching and supporting each other with their hands. They are now forming a bridge.

3. Pushing off each other, the players return to their original positions. Each player then moves back two inches, and the game continues as above.

4. The object is always for the players to catch and support each other as they fall. They can move as far apart as feels comfortable for them.

🍎 Despite its rather hair-raising appearance, this game offers very little opportunity for anyone to get hurt. Keep a watchful eye on things, however.

Blizzard[4]

Grades K–5

Procedure:

1. Have the kids find partners. One of the partners is blindfolded, and the other gently leads him or her through an imaginary snowstorm, over drifts, across frozen streams, around boulders, and past any other imaginary obstacles you place in the way.

2. Always stress to the leaders that they must be thoughtful and gentle in their leading.

🍎 With younger children, you may want to omit the blindfold and just have them close their eyes.

Taxi!

Grades 3–6

Procedure:

1. Students work in threes. Two of the kids form a seat with their hands, and the third hops aboard the taxi seat.

2. The two students who form the taxi seat either should be blindfolded or should just close their eyes. The rider then gives directions about

where he or she wants the taxi to go. Try this in an open space first; then add obstacles.

3. After a few minutes, the rider should become part of the taxi, giving another member of the trio a chance to ride.

Cooperative Musical Chairs[5]

Grades K-6   **Materials:** chairs, music source

Procedure:
1. In this version of musical chairs, the group wins or loses. Set up as for the traditional version, with one fewer chair than the number of players.

2. Play music, and stop it unexpectedly. Everyone tries to get a seat. The group is responsible for seeing that everyone has a place to sit, even if it's on someone's lap. Start the music again and remove one of the chairs. No one is eliminated.

3. Continue playing the music, stopping the music, and eliminating only chairs as you go along. Everyone sits on however many chairs are left, and everyone is responsible for helping the others stay on. If anyone falls, the group loses and must start again.

People of the Mountain[6]

Grades K-6   **Procedure:**

This is a cooperative version of king of the mountain, the traditional game in which one person tries to keep everyone else off a hill. The object instead here is to get as many people as possible on a hill, with no one falling off. If there's no hill or snowbank handy, a milk crate, chair, or very low desk will do.

Lap Sitting

Grades K-6   **Procedure:**
1. Have students form a circle, shoulder to shoulder. Have everyone face to the right and then take a side step toward the center of the circle to tighten it up.

2. When everyone is pressed together in a tight circle, give instructions to sit at the count of three. Each player sits on the lap of the player behind.

Tug of Peace

Grades K-6   **Materials:** long rope, tied to form a large circle

Procedure:
Lay the rope out in a circle. Have students seat themselves around it and grab hold. Explain that the object of the game is for all the members of the group to raise themselves to a standing position by pulling on the rope. If anyone falls, the group loses. Count to three and say, "Go!" (It's harder than it sounds!)

Spider Web

Grades K–3

Procedure:

1. Have some of the students hold hands in lines of four or five. These are the spider webs. There should be one extra child for each web. These are the flies.

2. The webs chase the flies. When the beginning or the end of the web touches the fly, the fly is caught and the web wraps itself around him or her. The fly is now part of the web.

3. The last person in the web then breaks free and becomes a new fly.

Inventing Games

Grades K–6

Procedure:

Kids enjoy inventing new games, and inventing a cooperative game is a wonderful exercise in building community. The guidelines listed at the beginning of this section are a good place to start. They outline the kind of game you want, one where everyone can participate and have fun.

The game creators need to answer the following questions (though not necessarily in this order):

What materials will we use in our game?

What is the goal of our game?

What must the players do to reach the goal?

How will the players cooperate?

Will everyone be involved?

Is the game interesting and fun?

Will everyone win?

In my own experience, once children have played cooperative games and have a familiarity with how they work, they really need very little help in developing new games.

For older children who might like to be more systematic about designing games, there are four principles, or goals, of cooperative games.[7]

1. *Simultaneous finish.* All players make the final move at the same time.

2. *Coordinated manipulation.* All players coordinate timing and movement with other group members so a smooth pattern of manipulation results.

3. *Rotation.* Each player takes a turn in sequence and is responsible for one indispensable step toward the final goal.

4. *Predetermined score.* Players combine efforts to reach a set score.

Balloon freeze (below) is a predetermined-score game developed by a kindergarten class I had a few years ago.

Balloon Freeze

Grades K–3   **Materials:** balloons

Procedure:

Have the children bounce balloons into the air as you count at a steady rate. They should try to hit the balloons only when you count. The object is for the class to reach fifty points. If someone misses, the class must freeze until all the balloons reach the floor. Then start over from one. The game can be made more difficult by speeding or slowing the counting.

New Games from Old

Grades 4–6   **Materials:** old game boards, game materials (dice, markers, blank cards, sticky labels)

Procedure:

1. Divide the class into groups of four. Give each group an old game board and set out game materials where they are accessible to all groups.

2. The task for each group is to take the game board and whatever materials they need and remake the game into a cooperative one. They are not bound by any aspect of the old game: they may make whatever changes they wish in the rules and the board.

3. When finished, the group should write a set of clear, new rules and give it to another group to test.

Discussion:

What's the goal of your new game?

What game principles did you use?

What was the hardest part of designing a new game?

Cooperation Activities

These activities involve your conscious effort to teach kids how to work together. They are, for the most part, process activities, unrelated to subject matter. This frees children from anxiety about getting right answers and allows them to concentrate on the group process skills involved. Once they have mastered these skills, they are ready to work cooperatively in academic areas.

I always begin teaching cooperation skills by having the kids work in groups of two and then three, four, and more as the year goes on and their skill increases. I also mix up the groups so that kids are frequently working with new kids.

As students participate in their groups, you should circulate through the room observing how they work together. Try to find both strengths and weaknesses to point out during later discussions. It is very likely that conflicts will arise during group work. Help the groups resolve them and point out any positive results from the conflicts. Then encourage the kids to get on with the task at hand.

Learning to cooperate takes time; and, at first, success in one activity won't necessarily carry over to another, especially with young children. Eventually, however, they will get it. You may have an experience similar to mine. One day when I was teaching kindergarten, two boys showed me a difficult puzzle they'd put together. As I congratulated them, one of the boys assured me, "It was a piece of cake. We cooperated."

Dividing into Groups

Grades K–6

Procedure:

1. Use what I call the barnyard method: choose animals (the number of animals you choose depends on how many groups you want and how big you want them to be) that make distinctive sounds, such as ducks, dogs, and cats. Whisper the name of an animal in each student's ear. The student then finds the others in his or her group by making the appropriate sound.

2. Draw names from a hat. Say, "Group one will be Sandra, Wayne, Alex, and Denise. Group two . . . ," etc.

3. Take a deck of playing cards, and decide how many groups you need. If you want five groups, take out all the aces, twos, threes, fours, and fives. Pile these together and shuffle well. Have the kids draw from the top of the deck; and then say, "All the aces over here; all the twos here," and so on. (Obviously, this method mandates groups of four.)

Totem Pole

Grades K–2

Materials: boxes, paint, white glue, art junk (paper scraps, cardboard tubes, fabric, spools, styrofoam)

Procedure:

1. Divide the children into groups of three or four. Give each group a box. The group should decide what color or colors to paint the box.

2. When the boxes have dried, set out the glue and junk materials. Have each group decide how they will make a face on the box, and how they will embellish it. When they have decided, they may begin working.

3. When all the groups are finished, stack the boxes, largest to smallest, to make a totem pole.

Discussion:

What part of the project did you like best?

How did you decide what your group would do?

Did you have problems in your group? How did you solve them?

🍎 Pictures of actual totem poles enhance this project and give the children ideas. (Before you try to tie this in to a unit on Native Americans, be sure the tribes you are studying had totems; not all did.)

Toothpicks

Grades K-6

Materials: toothpicks (about a thousand for twenty students)

Procedure:

1. Have the students work in pairs the first time you do this activity. Give each pair a pile of about fifty toothpicks.

2. The task is for the children to make some kind of creation from their toothpicks. Anything is acceptable—a design, a picture, a sculpture—whatever they can come up with. The only ground rules are that each person get a chance to help decide what the creation will be and that each person get a chance to help make it.

3. After fifteen minutes or so, have everyone stop. Give the class a chance to wander around the room and see what everyone has made.

4. Repeat this activity a number of times. Each time, increase the number of students in the group.

Discussion:

How did you decide what to make?

What problems did you encounter in deciding? How did you solve them?

What problems did you have with the materials? How did you solve them?

🍎 If students use white glue to affix the toothpicks to bases of tagboard or cardboard, the creations can be made permanent.

Monster Making[8]

Grades K-4, (5, 6)

Materials: paper, crayons, scissors

Procedure:

1. Have the students work in small groups. The task is to create a monster. There are only two ground rules, and they are that each person get a chance to help decide what the creation will be and that each person get a chance to help make it.

2. In addition to making the monster, the group should name it and make up a little of its life story. When all the groups have finished, have them share their monsters and the stories.

Discussion:

What problems did you encounter working together?

How did you resolve them?

🍎 Older kids can get involved in designing and making a larger monster and using a more sophisticated variety of materials.

Toothpicks-Monster Model

Grades K–6

Materials: see below

Procedure:

The basic format of the toothpicks and monster-making activities can be adapted to whatever materials you have at hand. Always state the goal of the activity clearly, and give the ground rules:

1. Everyone helps make decisions.
2. Everyone helps construct the project.

Some assignments I've found successful:

Make a puzzle with cardboard, crayons or markers, and scissors.

Make Tinker Toy inventions.

Make clay sculptures.

Make junk sculptures.

Make a mural (related, for instance, to social studies or science).

Coming to Consensus

Grades 2–6

Procedure:

1. Write "consensus" on the board. Explain that there is a consensus when a group comes to a decision that is acceptable to everyone, even if it is not everyone's first choice.
2. With the class, brainstorm a list of twenty-five or so possible field trips. Then have each person write down the five field trips on the list that he or she would like to take.
3. Put the students in groups of three. Have them come up with a list of four trips they would all like to take.
4. Combine groups so that there are groups of six. These groups should choose two trips by consensus.
5. These groups should then report to the class. Combine the lists, and have the whole class come to a consensus. (The logical follow-up is to take the field trip.)

Discussion:

What problems did you have coming to consensus?

How did you come to agreement? What were your reasons for your choices?

Peace Cranes, Cooperative and Competitive

Grades 3–6

Materials: lots of scrap paper

Procedure:

1. Teach the kids how to make origami cranes using the illustrated directions on pages 138 and 139. Let them practice by making a few cranes, and explain the Japanese legend that if one makes one thou-

sand paper cranes one's wish will come true. Say that the class will try to make one thousand paper cranes to see what happens.

2. Have a contest to see who can make the most cranes in twenty minutes. When the time is up, congratulate the winner, and count how many cranes the class as a whole made. Note that they are a long way from one thousand.

3. Group students by fours, and say that it will be interesting to see if crane making goes faster when they cooperate. Give the groups twenty minutes to make cranes; then stop the activity and count the cranes made.

4. The class will still be a ways from one thousand, so pin the existing cranes to a bulletin board, and set out scrap paper and pins for students to make more cranes to add to the display.

🍎 If your students are sufficiently mature, you might want to read the book *Sadako and the Thousand Paper Cranes* by Eleanor Coerr, which explains why paper cranes have come to be known as peace cranes.

Discussion:

What were some of the differences between cooperation and competition?

When might you want to use one or the other?

Kisses[9]

Grades 2–6

Materials: chocolate kisses or other small candies or grapes or peanuts or raisins

Procedure:

The point of this activity is to show that we often compete, even when it is against our best interests. In this activity, it is not against the rules to allow hands to touch the desk without resistance—but don't tell the kids that.

1. Have students choose partners and get into arm wrestling position; do not, however, use the term *arm wrestling*, because it denotes competition. If kids use the term, say that the position is the same, but the rules are different.

2. Once everyone is in position, explain the rules:

> You may not talk.
>
> You will receive one chocolate kiss each time the back of your partner's hand touches the desk.
>
> You must keep track of your own kisses.

Say "Begin!" and allow thirty seconds of play.

3. Students invariably compete at this. Stop the game after thirty seconds and discuss as below. Then replay cooperatively for fifteen seconds.

Constructing an Origami Crane

1. Take a square piece of lightweight paper, white or the same color on both sides, and fold it in half.

2. Fold it in half again.

3. Fold it again in half, and unfold.

4. Pick up the top sheet at the point and turn it outward and over, bringing point A to meet point B.

5. Turn the paper over, and repeat on the other side to create a box.

6. Fold the outside edges in so that the sides fall along the center line, and unfold. Fold the top down, making a crease, and unfold.

7. Lift C, folding along DE, so that the edges of the paper meet at the center line.

8. Turn the paper over, and repeat.

9. Fold the top layer on the dotted lines shown in 8 so that F and G meet at the center line.

10. Turn the paper over and repeat. Fold the bottom points up along the dotted lines, and unfold.

11. Lift point H to form the neck. (Fold the tip down to form the head.) Lift point I to form the tail.

12. Spread the large flaps to make wings, and blow air into the hole underneath to fill the body.

13. Your finished crane will look like this.

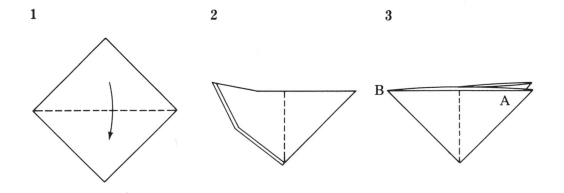

1   2   3

4

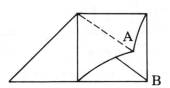

5

6

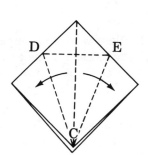

7

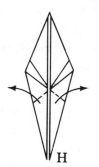

8

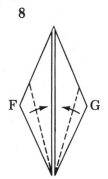

9

10

11

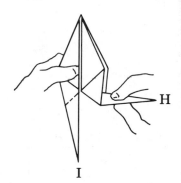

12

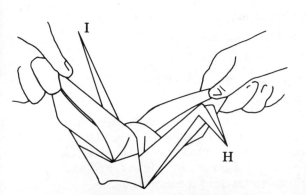

13

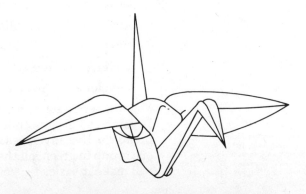

Discussion:

Why did you automatically compete?

What was the goal of the game?

Did the other person's gaining kisses mean you lost them?

What did you stand to gain by cooperation?

Are there other situations in which we compete without thinking?

Aboard the Mayflower[10]

Grades 2–6

Procedure:

This activity offers a chance to practice consensus.

1. Review the meaning of *consensus*. Have the class work in groups of three or four. Explain to the class that each group has a chance to go aboard the Mayflower and visit the New World. Because the Mayflower is small, the group can take only ten things with them, and they must be things that existed in 1620.

2. The groups should develop a list by consensus of the ten things they would like to take to the New World. Have groups read their lists aloud, and discuss problems that occurred.

Discussion:

What items could you easily agree on?

What criteria did you use for choosing things? (Often they use no criteria.)

What items were difficult to agree on?

How did you solve disagreements?

🍎 The format of this survival activity can be adapted to many different imaginary settings, e.g., desert island, new planet colony, lifeboat.

Busted Sentences[11]

Grades 3–6

Materials: five envelopes for each group, word cards (see below)

Procedure:

Prepare envelopes with word cards in them as follows:

envelope 1: Spring, begun, eager, into

envelope 2: here, blinded, have, dashed, the

envelope 3: is, The, start, reading, The

envelope 4: sunlight, barking, I'm, cat, house

envelope 5: The, me, dogs, to

You will need a set of envelopes, one through five, for each group playing. If you can't group students exactly into groups of five, just give each group the five envelopes anyway. It helps to write all the word cards for one group in green, all the cards for another group in red, and so on. This will make it easier for you to keep track of the materials.

Adapted by permission of A&W Publishers, Inc. from *Developing Effective Classroom Groups* by Gene Stanford. Copyright © 1977, Hart Publishing Company, Inc.

1. Distribute envelopes to each group. Explain that each group is to construct five complete sentences without talking, gesturing, or signaling in any way. The only way to get a needed word is to have it passed to you by a group member.

2. Have the groups begin while you circulate as an observer. Interrupt if you see rule violations or signs of serious misunderstanding of the process. (In the latter case, nudge the group in the right direction.)

3. The sentences should be more or less these:

   Spring is here.

   The sunlight blinded me.

   The dogs have begun barking.

   I'm eager to start reading.

   The cat dashed into the house.

Discussion:

Did you keep an eye out for people in your group who needed help?

How did it feel when someone helped you? Didn't help you?

What did you learn from this activity?

Mystery Games[12]

Grades 2–6

Materials: clue cards (see below)

Procedure:

Mystery games require groups of students to pool information and come up with a predetermined answer to a mystery. Mystery games can be oriented toward either process or subject matter and involve either the whole class or small groups. As a rule, it is best to begin with small groups. In any case, the procedure is the same:

1. Distribute clues typed on three-by-five-inch index cards.

2. Every child should have a clue. If there aren't enough clues, divide the class into two or more groups, or add dummy clues. If there are extra clues, give some students more than one.

3. Explain, "Each of you has a clue which may or may not be useful in solving the mystery. Consider all the information, and try to come to consensus on an answer. You may not show anyone else your card; you may only read it aloud."

4. Add any instructions or background information appropriate to the specific mystery you are using.

5. Tell the group that you will time them, and have them begin. You may choose to help or not. Observe the group interaction, noting carefully what is helpful behavior and what is not. If they get hopelessly muddled after ten minutes, steer them in the right direction. If necessary, walk them through the mystery, assuring them that they will get better as they solve more mysteries.

Adapted by permission of A&W Publishers, Inc. from *Developing Effective Classroom Groups* by Gene Stanford. Copyright © 1977, Hart Publishing Company, Inc.

Discussion:

How did you deal with everyone's talking at once?

How did you organize yourselves?

Did you need a leader?

Was everyone involved in solving the mystery?

Did some people not want to share their clues?

 Add your observations to the discussion.

Five Evil Dragons

Grades 3–6

Materials: clue cards (see mystery games activity, above)

Procedure:

See the mystery games instructions, above. This is a mystery game for the whole class.

Say, "Once there were five evil dragons. Their names were Jason, Meredith, Alex, Joanna, and George. They had captured Princess Patty and held her prisoner, tied at the wrists and ankles with ropes. Now she has escaped. The dragons suspect each other of having helped her. Your task is to determine how Patty escaped; who, if anyone, helped her; and why."

Pass out clue cards:

Jason and Meredith breathe fire.

Blue scales were found near the stake.

Princess Patty had been tied to the stake for twenty-one days.

Princess Patty was very thin.

Yellow scales were found near the stake.

Alex and Jason have yellow scales down their backs.

Joanna and George have blue scales down their backs.

Joanna and Meredith have just returned from an all-day raiding party at a nearby village.

Nothing was charred in the vicinity of the stake.

George prefers to eat plump peasants.

All the ropes but one were untied.

One rope was cut.

Meredith and Jason are hungry for royalty.

Alex likes to burn his food to a crisp.

Joanna will devour anything.

Jason was supposed to be standing guard, but he fell asleep.

A dragon's claws are as sharp as knives.

The dragons have eaten many princes and princesses in the past few months.

If you have more than twenty students, add dummy clues, such as:

Joanna and Meredith brought back gold and jewels.

Alex is afraid Patty will return with an army.

Meredith's scales are slimy.

The solution to the mystery is that George helped Princess Patty escape by cutting one of her ropes, because he was tired of eating skinny princesses.

Cooperative Learning

Cooperative learning has many benefits for your classroom. Not only can it improve relationships and reduce conflicts, it can also engage students who previously were uninterested in academics. Jean Piaget tells us that interaction is a most important aspect of learning, and research shows that children in cooperative learning situations do academically as well as or better than students in competitive or individualized programs.

I want to emphasize that I am not talking about an all-or-nothing choice. It's not necessary to have students cooperate all the time. In fact, a judicious blend of cooperative, individual, and competitive approaches is probably the most effective. The chart on pages 144 and 145 will help you choose the most appropriate structure for a particular activity.

Evaluate cooperative learning as you would any other, by observation, discussion, tests, quizzes, etc. Students learning cooperatively needn't be tested cooperatively. Always make it clear that each individual is responsible for knowing the material.

Assessing Process

Grades K–6

Procedure:

Once students are used to working in cooperative groups, you don't have to focus quite so much on the process of working cooperatively, but you should bring it up regularly to help students stay aware of it. And certainly you should discuss process whenever problems arise. Some of the following questions are useful:

What did you learn from this activity?

How did you share work?

How did you share ideas?

What problems, if any, arose?

How did you solve them?

Older students (grades two through six) can develop a process assessment checklist. Discuss helpful cooperative behavior that might be noted on a checklist, and then have the students work in groups to develop such a list. Combine the results, and duplicate a form that can be used to assess the quality of group process skills during cooperative activities.

Appropriate Conditions for Cooperative, Individualized, and Competitive Learning[13]

	Cooperative
Type of Instructional Activity	Problem solving; divergent thinking or creative tasks; assignments can be more ambiguous with students doing the clarifying, decision making, and inquiring.
Perception of Goal Importance	Goal is perceived as important for each student, and students expect group to achieve the goal.
Student Expectations	Each student expects positive interaction with other students, sharing of ideas and materials, support for risk taking, making contributions to the group effort, dividing the task among group members, to capitalize on diversity among group members.
Expected Source of Support	Other students are perceived to be the major resource for assistance, support, and reinforcement.

David W. Johnson, Roger T. Johnson, *Learning Together and Alone: Cooperation, Competition and Individualization,* © 1975, p. 62. Reprinted by permission of Prentice-Hall, Inc., Englewood Cliffs, N.J.

Historical Cooperation

Grades 3–6

Materials: reference materials

Procedure:

1. Divide students into groups. Assign each group a historical time and place to research, such as ancient China, pre-Columbian Inca civilization, Renaissance Italy, or a period the class is studying.

2. Have each group research their period and uncover five examples of cooperation among the people living at that time. These can be presented to the class through a variety of means, including written or oral reports, models, and bulletin boards.

Discussion:

How did you find examples?

What examples were similar to current ones? Different?

Are some examples more or less cooperative than others?

Individualized	*Competitive*
Specific skill or knowledge acquisition; assignment is clear and behavior specified to avoid confusion and need for extra help.	Skill practice; knowledge recall and review; assignment is clear with rules for competing specified.
Goal is perceived as important for each student, and each student expects eventually to achieve his or her goal.	Goal is not perceived to be of large importance to the students, and they can accept either winning or losing.
Each student expects to be left alone by other students, to take a major part of the responsibility for completing the task, to take a major part in evaluating his progress toward task completion and the quality of his or her effort.	Each student expects to have an equal chance of winning, to enjoy the activity (win or lose), to monitor the progress of competitors, to compare ability, skills, or knowledge with peers'.
Teacher is perceived to be the major resource for assistance, support, and reinforcement.	Teacher is perceived to be the major resource for assistance, support and reinforcement.

Subject Matter Mysteries

Grades 1-6

Procedure:

These are mystery games for small groups.

1. To first through third graders, say, "What character am I, and from what book?" Give them the clues:

    I am not a human being.

    I live on the Island of Nantucket.

    My friend in the book is a boy.

    My friend spills flour on the way home from the miller's.

    The author of the book is Brinton Turkle.

    The answer is the seagull in *Thy Friend Obadiah*.

2. To third or fourth graders, say, "What country is this? What is its capital?" Give them the clues:

    It is located in Europe.

It gave the United States the Statue of Liberty.

It is famous for good wine and food.

Famous landmarks in it include Chartres, the Eiffel Tower, and Notre Dame.

Its language gave us such words or phrases as *en route, liqueur,* and *massage*.

The country is France; its capital is Paris.

3. To fifth or sixth graders, say, "What does the word *alleviate* mean?" Give them the clues:

Patty wants to *alleviate* herself of her chores at home.

We *alleviated* the wheelbarrow load by removing the rocks.

Hank is *alleviating* me of some of my heavy books.

I wish someone would *alleviate* my homework tonight!

A good secretary *alleviates* the boss of some paperwork.

Other subject matter mystery topics include:

What [city, state, country]?

What famous [current, historical] person?

What bodily organ?

What heavenly body?

What number?

What [animal, plant, rock, dinosaur]?

Problem-solving Groups

Grades K–6

Procedure:

Problem-solving groups differ from mystery games or subject matter mystery groups in that they have no predetermined answer and usually no single right answer. Just give small groups a problem to solve, and explain the ground rules, which are that everyone help make decisions and that everyone contribute in some way to the final product.

This leaves the means entirely up to the students and makes a big demand of the group. Use your judgment as to whether or not your class is ready for this. Monitor the groups as they work to help with problems that arise.

Here are some problems you might present:

Make a list of place names that begin with every letter of the alphabet.

Design a better ———.

Write a skit in a fairy-tale format.

Develop a democratic government for a make-believe planet.

Write a story that includes all our spelling and vocabulary words for the week.

Alphabet Activities

Grades 2–5

Materials: ditto with all the letters of the alphabet going down the left side, with a blank line following each letter

Procedure:

1. Divide students into groups. Give each *student* an alphabet sheet. Give each *group* a globe.

2. Have them find the name of a place for each letter of the alphabet. Each student must fill out his or her own sheet, but the group can and should work together. As students write the names, they should add the following symbols:

continent	+
country	$
state	✔
city or town	☆

3. This activity can be adapted in a number of ways: students can write and research people's names, book titles, animal names, five-letter words, and so on. This is a great end-of-the-day, relax-a-little activity that kids really enjoy.

Discussion:

How did your group divide up the work?

What were the most difficult letters to fill in?

Word Chains

Grades 1–4, (5, 6)

Materials: pencils, paper

Procedure:

1. For this vocabulary-building activity, students should work in groups of two or three—larger groups become unwieldy. On a piece of paper, the first student writes a word and then passes the paper and pencil to the second student.

2. The second student writes a word that begins with the final letter of the first word (for instance, if the first word was *animal*, the second might be *letter*) and passes it either to the third person (if there is one) or back to the first. The length of the list is variable. Start with twenty words.

🍎 For older students, add another requirement. The word must not only begin with the final letter of the previous word; it must somehow relate to the concept of the previous word, e.g., *car, racing, gallop, pony.*

Group Stories

Grades 3–6

Materials: pencils, paper

Procedure:

1. Divide the class into groups of three or four. The task is for each group to write a paragraph that begins a story by setting the scene,

introducing two main characters, and stating their problem. The groups have five minutes to do this.

2. After five minutes, the paragraph is passed on to the next group, which has five minutes to continue the story. At the end of this time, the story is passed to the next group, which also continues the story; and finally it is passed to the next group, which has five minutes to come up with an ending. The group that develops the ending should read the story to the class.

Discussion:

What roles did people in your group play?

Did everyone get a chance to contribute in some way?

What was the most difficult part of this activity?

Grammar Circles

Grades 2–5

Materials: one envelope for each group, each envelope containing five green circles, five red circles, and five yellow circles with the following words on them:

green: animals, running, she, but, beautiful

red: telephone, flow, him, about, angry

yellow: radio, listens, I, to, sunny

Procedure:

1. Give each group an envelope. Someone should open the envelope and give each group member three circles, one of each color. The object is for each group member to collect three circles with the same part of speech on them: noun, verb, pronoun, adjective, preposition.

2. The ground rules are the same as for busted sentences. No one may speak, gesture, or in any way signal. Group members must see that someone needs a particular circle and voluntarily give it to him or her.

● This activity is infinitely variable. It can be used for any categorizing or sorting activity.

Buying Candy

Grades 2–4

Procedure:

1. Describe to the children the following situation: Five friends walk up to a candy machine. The machine does not give change; it accepts only the exact amount of purchase. The only way to get change is from friends.

2. Write on the board:

All candies cost twenty cents.

Matt has no money.

Mitzi has a quarter and a nickel.

Lisa has two dimes and two nickels.

Chris has three nickels.

Emmy has two dimes.

3. Divide the class into groups (of five, if possible). Have each group figure out how many candy bars can be bought, what to do with them when they have bought them, and what to do with leftover change.

The Peace Team

Grades 4–6

Materials: peace team cards (see Appendix), paper, pencils

Procedure:

1. Divide the class into groups. Explain that each group is a peace team, summoned to make peace in a particular situation. The group must work together to develop a solution to the problem situation in a limited amount of time. The consequences of not doing so will be dire. The solution must be written and submitted with the situation card.

2. Pass out the situation cards, one face down before each group. Each group should receive a description of a different problem. At a signal, give each peace team three minutes to submit a solution. The consequences are listed on the cards.

3. Read the problem cards aloud along with the solutions. Discuss the solutions. If a group didn't finish, don't read its peace team card; just wish it better luck next time.

4. Continue as above, but give less and less time (or if your class needs it, you can, of course, give more time).

Discussion:

How did your group reach a decision?

What would help you do it more quickly?

What things slowed you down?

Jigsaw Groups

Grades 4–6

Procedure:

The jigsaw approach to cooperative learning was developed by psychologist Elliot Aronson and his colleagues. The process of jigsaw grouping is somewhat similar to that used in mystery games. The following instructions give the general idea. They assume groups of five (you may need to adapt them).

1. Take a specific topic, such as how the United Nations is organized.

2. Divide the topic into five parts, one for each child in the group. In the example, one child might learn about the operation of the General Assembly, another the Secretariat, and so on. Supply each student with the material he or she needs.

3. Each student is then responsible for studying the information he or she was given. However, all the students in the group are responsible for knowing all the material. This means that they must work

together, teach each other what they know, ask questions, and help each other.

4. At the end of the lesson (the length of which will vary), test the students individually for an individual grade.

🍎 The jigsaw approach has limitations: it's difficult to use with young children, and it's difficult to use in some subject areas. However, Aronson has conducted impressive and convincing research concerning the academic and interpersonal progress of students who use the jigsaw approach. I highly recommend his book *The Jigsaw Classroom* (see Bibliography of Resources).

Notes

1. Linden Nelson and Spencer Kagen, "Competition, the Star-Spangled Scramble," *Psychology Today*, September 1972, p. 91.

2. Excellent summaries of current research on cooperation and competition in schools can be found in David Johnson and Roger Johnson, *Learning Together and Alone* (Englewood Cliffs, N.J.: Prentice-Hall, 1975) and Elliot Aronson et al., *The Jigsaw Classroom* (Beverly Hills, Calif.: Sage, 1978).

3. I learned this game from Sandy Eccleston.

4. From *The Cooperative Sports and Games Book* by Terry Orlick. Copyright © 1978 by Terry Orlick. Reprinted by permission of Pantheon Books, a Division of Random House, Inc.

5. I learned this game from Sandy Eccleston.

6. From *The Second Cooperative Sports and Games Book* by Terry Orlick. Copyright © 1982 by Terry Orlick. Reprinted by permission of Pantheon Books, a Division of Random House, Inc.

7. I learned these cooperative game principles from Sukie Rice.

8. Priscilla Prutzman et al., *The Friendly Classroom for a Small Planet* (Wayne, N.J.: Avery, 1978), pp. 24–25. Reprinted by permission of the publisher.

9. Educators for Social Responsibility, *A Day of Dialogue: Planning and Curriculum Resource Guide* (Boston, 1982). Used with permission.

10. I learned this acitivity from Birgit Arons.

11. Adapted by permission of A&W Publishers, Inc. from *Developing Effective Classroom Groups* by Gene Stanford. Copyright © 1977, Hart Publishing Co., Inc.

12. Adapted by permission of A&W Publishers, Inc. from *Developing Effective Classroom Groups* by Gene Stanford. Copyright © 1977, Hart Publishing Co., Inc.

13. David W. Johnson, Roger T. Johnson, *Learning Together and Alone: Cooperation, Competition and Individualization,* © 1975, p. 62. Reprinted by permission of Prentice-Hall, Inc., Englewood Cliffs, N.J.

Chapter 8

Teaching Tolerance

The most universal quality is diversity.
—Montaigne

Harriet Welsch, that feisty eleven-year-old Samuel Pepys of the children's classic *Harriet the Spy*, once noted in her journal: "I think I made up a good moral—that is that some people are one way and some people are another, and that's that."[1]

No one could argue the truth of Harriet's moral, but the implications of it have caused a multitude of problems. For over two hundred years, American society has tried, with varying degrees of success, to balance a highly diverse group of people and cultures. This unique diversity has given the United States its vitality and cultural richness. The conflicts arising from this cultural pluralism have provided some of the finest and some of the most shameful times in our history.

It would seem logical, then, that learning to tolerate and appreciate diversity would be an essential part of a child's education. Yet a look at the headlines and the nightly news seems to indicate that we are rapidly losing our tolerance for diversity, our appreciation for the differences that have enriched our culture. Racism, prejudice, discrimination, and

151

simple lack of respect for one another continue to be among our most pressing social problems.

No one needs to tell you what diversity exists in your classroom. Even if you stand before a sea of faces of the same color each morning, there are still ethnic, religious, economic, value, and interest differences among your students. These differences can enrich your classroom, but they can also fuel conflict. Conflicts often occur along racial, ethnic, or religious lines. And conflicts between values are so common that they are classified in their own category. Differences do not, in and of themselves, cause classroom conflicts. It is the lack of tolerance for differences that can either cause conflicts or be used as fuel to escalate conflicts. I'm sure you've seen it many times: the intolerance and prejudice against differences on the part of some students, directed toward the child or children who present an easy target for teasing, scapegoating, or even worse. Where does all this intolerance come from?

How Prejudice and Intolerance Develop[2]

Much research has been conducted in the areas of prejudice and diversity; still, no one is exactly sure how prejudice develops in children, or why some people welcome diversity as enriching while others view it as threatening. We do know that children develop awareness of and prejudices against people who are different very early. These awarenesses or prejudices are reinforced by family, peer groups, societal and governmental institutions, and language.

Exercise

Racial groups are commonly described as red, yellow, black, and white. Try listing the various meanings and common expressions that involve these terms. Put a plus or minus sign next to each expression, depending on whether the term has a positive or negative connotation.

Which words have overwhelmingly negative connotations?

Which words have overwhelmingly positive ones?

This exercise shows how firmly prejudicial attitudes are rooted in our language. They are also rooted in other aspects of our culture, going back hundreds of years.

Exercise

Think of the European folk and fairy tales you know that have disabled characters. List the stories and characters. How many of the stories portray the disabled as heroic, noble, good, intelligent, or independent? In how many are the disable represented as evil, stupid, or servile?

Of course, race and physical disability are only two of the objects of this sort of ingrained cultural prejudice. Similar exercises could point out similar prejudices based on sex, religion, sexual orientation, ethnicity, and more. The purpose here is not necessarily to point out against whom the prejudice is directed; rather, it is to show that stereotypes and prejudice are pervasive and easily accessible through the common culture. This plays a role in the development of prejudicial attitudes, for children and adults tend to be as prejudiced and intolerant as the situation they are in allows.

A child seems to develop prejudice against a given group because of a bad experience with a member of the group. This experience can be direct or vicarious (through books, TV, or parental warnings). The child generalizes about the whole group on the basis of the experience. Then the available stereotypes plug into the child's poor image of the group, and not just the stereotypes, either; a whole batch of attitudes, purported evidence, and so-called common wisdom are included in the package. Once a prejudice even begins to form, it becomes a part of the child's perceptual framework. At this point, evidence supporting the prejudice enters the child's consciousness; and, for the most part, evidence that contradicts the prejudice is discarded.

Reducing Prejudice and Increasing Tolerance

There is, unfortunately, no surefire way to reduce students' prejudices and to cause them magically to achieve tolerance. Research in this area is inconclusive, but it does offer us some substantial clues with which to work. Merely presenting information about ethnic or minority groups, for example, seems to effect little or no change in student attitudes. On the other hand, contact with ethnic group members in a positive and cooperative context does seem to improve attitudes.

One teacher told me of inviting a Chinese woman from the community to her first grade classroom to demonstrate Chinese cooking. The teacher was mortified at the casual racist remarks the children made. The Chinese woman was also concerned; and, together, they planned an approach. The teacher worked with the children on understanding such concepts as stereotyping, generalizing, and name-calling. The Chinese woman continued to visit the classroom and to present different aspects of Chinese culture. During a culminating trip to Chinatown, the teacher reported that she heard not one racist or derogatory remark.

There is evidence, too, that children who are more sophisticated in such cognitive skills as problem solving and concept formation are less likely to exhibit prejudiced attitudes and behavior. As author-educator David Shiman states, "At a very basic level, it appears that schools can more effectively combat prejudice if they simply do a better job of educating."[3]

Also, research indicates, with striking regularity, that people who feel good about themselves and have strong, healthy self-concepts are much less likely to be prejudiced or intolerant than others. The implications for teachers are clear. Not only should we try to enhance student self-concepts, we must stress that putting down another person or group of people does not enhance one's prestige or sense of self or make one worthwhile.

Working with differences on a smaller scale in the classroom is also important. For example, how about the boy who hates baseball? Or the girl who builds model cars? Children are frequently fearful or condemning of such differences because they are either confusing or somehow threatening. The children may simply never have encountered much diversity before. They need to see concrete evidence of the value of diversity. You might provide opportunities for the boy or girl in the example to show that they too enrich the classroom. It is helpful to be very explicit with your students. Say clearly such things as, "Do you see how the differences in our class make it more interesting?" and "How does Ms. Chung contradict stereotypes of Asian-Americans?" Gently and tactfully, point out generalizing and stereotyping when they occur, and help the children understand what they are doing. You must be discreet about this, however. No good purpose is served by pointing a finger and accusing, "You're stereotyping!" or "You're prejudiced!" Such statements will only elicit defensive reactions.

Teacher Behavior

Whether or not people hold intolerant or prejudiced attitudes often depends on the prevailing attitudes in the group to which they belong. In other words, if tolerance is the norm in your milieu, you will, in all likelihood, become (or remain) pretty tolerant yourself.

That brings up an interesting question. How tolerant of diversity are you in your classroom? Must students toe a strict line, or does pretty much anything go, or are you somewhere in between? Now, obviously there have to be limits. Some kinds of diversity (for instance, disruptive behavior) can't be allowed. Here are some ways you can value constructive diversity in your classroom without sacrificing control.

1. Give students some choices in what they do. This need not cover every aspect of your curriculum, but try at some point each day to give options. For example, in my classroom children have a certain amount of required work every day in reading, writing, spelling, and math. Each day, one of these assignments involves a choice. Monday's math assignment might be a page in the math book or a game or a taped lesson. Tuesday's spelling assignment might be a crossword puzzle, a game, or a workbook page. The content taught in the options is the same; but the children get some, albeit very limited, choice in how it gets learned. A more ambitious approach is to negotiate a learning contract with each child on a daily or weekly basis. The contract states what the child will accomplish, and by what deadline. The child then takes responsibility for how and when she or he does the work. I admit that neither of these methods gives students a lot of choice. They do give some, however, and reflect a recognition that people have different ways of accomplishing what they must do.

2. Every day, use some open-ended acitivity somewhere in your curriculum. Our emphasis on obtaining the right answer often gives students the mistaken impression that there is always a single correct way of doing things. Use open-ended activities and be supportive of a

variety of responses to demonstrate that there is more than one way to accomplish things. Many of the activities in this book, particularly in chapter seven, are open-ended.

3. Next time a student asks, "Can I do it this way instead?" think before you say no. I frequently catch myself starting to say no for no good reason. When you get right down to it, is there any reason Julie can't add that extra fillip to her *y* during handwriting? Is there any reason Jacob can't use colored pencils instead of black pencil on his spelling words? Although there are sometimes very good reasons for saying "No, do it the way I said," often you'll find that there are not.

4. Provide opportunities for students to make contributions to the class that reflect their differences. I once had a boy who collected international dolls. As you might imagine, this led to a fair amount of teasing. It abruptly stopped the day I had him bring his collection in and share it with the class. A highly verbal child, he gave us a presentation that lasted over thirty minutes and held the children and myself spellbound. This approach doesn't always work so dramatically, but it is worth the effort to find creative ways to have children share their interests with the rest of the class. Childen often condemn diversity in others because they don't understand it. Once they understand and appreciate its value, their intolerance often drops by the wayside.

5. Take the time to point out the value of diversity. Don't lecture the class, but mention diversity in positive ways. "I like the way all our witches look so different." "I notice that this group came up with a very unusual way to solve the problem." In a similar vein, it helps to use stock phrases to remind the class of the value of diversity. "It takes all kinds to make up the world." "Everybody has his or her own way." "You can't fit a square peg into a round hole."

6. Be aware of how you treat different students. This is a sensitive subject, because you have to examine your own behavior, attitudes, prejudices, likes, and dislikes. The following questions may help you gain some insight:

> Which students are most like you? Least like you?
>
> Whom do you like best? Dislike most?
>
> Of whom are you most aware? Least aware?
>
> Who is most different from the others? How do you provide for him or her?
>
> Whom do you touch the most? Why?
>
> Whom do you never touch? Why?

Do patterns emerge as you answer these questions? These patterns can reflect your attitudes toward differences in general and different students in particular. It is through your behavior that your attitudes are passed on to students. Are you prejudiced and discriminatory toward students on the basis of arbitrary (and meaningless) differences? Only you can answer that question. The time such self-examination takes is well spent.

This chapter contains two activity sections:

Difference Activities

Prejudice Activities

Difference Activities

These activities deal with differences in both a general and a specific sense. They will help you explore and creatively use the diversity that exists in your classroom, and help set a tone of tolerance and mutual respect. (The activities at the end of chapter five are also helpful.)

Emphasize that an atmosphere of tolerance benefits everyone. With all the stress placed on difference in these activities, you should not neglect to point out similarities. The point here is not to place differences above similarities but rather to emphasize that differences have value.

The Universal Quality

Grades 3–6

Procedure:

Read the quote from the French philosopher Montaigne:

There never was in the world two opinions alike,
No more than two hairs or two grains.
The most universal quality is diversity.

Discussion:

What does *diversity* mean? What does *universal* mean?

What is Montaigne saying?

Do you agree?

What about the first line? Is that true? (You may need to explain the concept of hyperbole.)

In what ways is diversity good?

In what ways might it be bad?

What effect might diversity have on conflict?

How do you respond to people who are like you? Somewhat different? Very different?

The Human Family

Grades K–2

Materials: drawing paper, crayons, magazines, scissors, paste

Procedure:

1. Have the children draw pictures of their families and label family members. Post these on a bulletin board, and add photographs of

family groupings that may not appear in drawings (e.g., single-parent families, childless couples). Discuss the differences and similarities.

2. Tell the children that they also belong to a much larger family, the human family. Distribute magazines and scissors and have the class cut out pictures of people to paste into a collage of the human family.

3. Discuss the diversity of the human family. Try to come up with a definition or description of a human.

Discussion:

How many people are in your family?

Who has the most people? Who has the least?

Does anyone know a family with no children?

Does anyone have grandparents or other relatives besides parents and siblings living with him or her?

Look at all the different kinds of people in the human family:

How do they differ?

How are they similar?

Where might some of these people live?

All Kinds of Families

Grades K–2

Materials: magazines, scissors, paste, paper

Procedure:

Have the children cut out pictures of people from the magazines until they have a pile of ten or so. Then have them mount the pictures on the paper in family units. Encourage them to create as many types of families —single-parent, extended, interracial—as they can.

Discussion:

How are these families like yours?

How are they different?

What do all families need?

Face to Face

Grades (K, 1), 2–6

Procedure:

1. Assign partners and have them stand or sit facing each other. Everyone has three minutes to find out and jot down five ways he or she differs from his or her partner, and five characteristics they have in common.

2. When three minutes are up, everyone changes partners and repeats the exercise.

3. With the entire class, list the typical similarities and differences on the board.

Discussion:

What were some of the differences?

Were there similarities that went along with the differences (e.g., everyone has hair, but hair has different colors and textures)?

Which differences are most important? Least important?

Did you notice mostly physical characteristics?

What other characteristics could you have noticed?

What features are most people born with?

Which can they change? How?

🍎 Try having young children brainstorm lists of physical similarities and differences.

Three Musketeers

Grades 2–6

Materials: three musketeers sheet (see Appendix)

Procedure:

1. Students should work in groups of three. Distribute one worksheet to each group.

2. In the first section of the worksheet, the group should list three things that all the members of the group like; in the second, three things they all dislike.

3. In the third section, each group member should describe one way he or she differs from the other group members.

Discussion:

How did you decide what you liked and disliked?

Were there any groups that couldn't come to agreement?

What were some of your responses?

What does the phrase *all for one and one for all* mean?

Comparisons

Grades 3–6

Materials: comparisons worksheet (see Appendix)

Procedure:

1. Distribute the worksheet, and have the students complete it.

2. Have students find someone in class with at least three answers the same as their own. Have each student put the other's name on the paper and circle the items on which they agree. Give the students five minutes to discuss the items on which they disagree.

3. Have students write a paragraph on the back of the worksheet saying how they are similar and how they are different from their partners.

🍎 As a variation, randomly group students in threes and proceed as described above.

Discussion:

Why do people have different preferences?

What makes cheerfulness in a friend very important to some people and not as important to others?

Did you learn anything new about someone?

We Need Differences

Grades 1–4

Materials: three-by-five-inch index cards, pencils

Procedure:

1. Have the students pretend they are going to take a trip to Mars. Ask, "If you could have one person with you, what *kind* of person would it be?" Have students write their responses on three-by-five cards.

2. Have students read their responses and say why that type of person would be a good companion. For example, kids might choose:

   a person good with tools

   a good cook

   someone who knows about camping

   a good storyteller

   Write the responses on the board.

Discussion:

Would it be good to be on Mars with only people who were alike?

Very few of these descriptions have anything to do with looks. How important are differences in appearance?

Why does our world need differences?

Looking at Differences, Plus and Minus

Grades K–6

Procedure:

1. Explain that, in many cases, differences can be seen as positive or negative, depending on one's point of view. Say, "Suppose we had a child in our room who was in a wheelchair," assuming no such child is in your class. "What might be positive about her or his presence?" Have the class come up with three pluses. "What might be negative?" Have the class name three minuses. Finally, have the class name three ways it would make no difference at all.

2. Continue the exercise with examples appropriate for your class. You might try the following:

   a non-English-speaking child

   a deaf child

   a blind teacher

   a black teacher with an all-white class

Discussion:

Why do we sometimes see differences as positive at one time and negative at another?

How can we emphasize the positive?

If we have strong negative feelings about a particular difference, what can we do?

Being Different

Grades (1), 2–6

Procedure:

1. Discuss with the class when they've felt different, how it felt, and so on. The discussion will probably focus on the negative aspects of feeling different.

2. Say, "Everyone is different sometimes. This isn't necessarily bad. There are often some very good things about being different." Encourage the class to mention some of the positive aspects of being different.

Discussion:

What if you were the only boy or girl in the class? What would be good about that?

What if you were the only disabled person?

The only person of color?

The only kid who liked baseball?

The only person who forgot his or her lunch?

What would be good about it?

 Try mixing serious what-ifs with less serious ones.

Inheritances[4]

Grades (K, 1), 2–6

Materials: inheritances survey sheet (see Appendix), inked stamp pads

Procedure:

1. Discuss what physical characteristics are inherited. Explain that there might be some that children don't know about:

    tongue rolling

    dimples

    widow's peak

    hitchhiker's thumb

    attached vs. unattached earlobes

2. Distribute the inheritances survey. Ask why it includes space for fingerprints; what do they have to do with inherited characteristics? Give students time to complete the survey forms, and then discuss them.

🍎 With young children, omit the survey and conduct a class poll. Young children also enjoy comparing fingerprints. Teach them to make fingerprint pictures.

Physical Differences—Physical Disabilities[5]

Grades K-6

Procedure:

1. Ask if there are physical differences that affect what people can do. Answers will probably begin with height and strength differences, but eventually someone will mention physical disability. If not, nudge the students along.

2. List on the board all the disabilities that the children mention, and suggest those they forget. Discuss how the disabilities affect behavior.

3. To give the kids an opportunity to experience different disabilities, try the following:

   Play the blizzard game (see chapter seven) for blindness.

   Bring a pair of crutches or a wheelchair into the classroom.

   Tape the fingers of one hand of each student together and have each student try to pick things up.

   Place two tongue depressors in a student's mouth and have him or her try to talk clearly.

Discussion:

How did [*particular disability*] limit what you could do?

What things could you still do?

Physical Differences—Skin Color

Grades K-6

Materials: pictures of people with different-colored skin

Procedure:

1. Display the pictures. Ask students to label the skin color of each person. Ask, "Is black skin really black? Is white skin really white?" Ask, "Why is skin different colors?"

2. Have older students research skin color individually or in groups and write reports about it.

3. For young children, here is a simple explanation: "The sun's rays could be dangerous to people's skin, so skin has something to protect it. It has tiny dark specks called melanin. Melanin absorbs the sun's rays so skin won't burn as easily as without melanin. When you suntan, your skin gets darker because melanin is coming to the surface of your skin to protect it from the sun. Different people have different amounts of melanin. In these pictures, who do you think has the most? The least?"

Discussion:

Does the amount of melanin have anything to do with a person's behavior?

Does the amount of melanin make anyone better or worse than anyone else?

What determines how much melanin is in the skin?

Pick Your Corner

Grades K–6

Procedure:

1. Designate one corner of the room as the belonging corner, another as the not-belonging corner.

2. Have the class stand. When you say the name of a group, the children who belong to that group should go to the appropriate corner. Those who do not should go to the opposite corner. Repeat the procedure with several group names. Possible groups are: girls, not girls; cub scouts, not cub scouts; tall, not tall; Christian, not Christian; bike riders, not bike riders; Italian, not Italian. The groups you name can be as controversial (or noncontroversial) as you wish, depending in part on the age and maturity of your class and in part on the type of discussion with which you wish to follow the assignment to corners.

Discussion:

What is a group?

What were some of the groups you belonged to?

Which groups were you born into? Which did you join?

Why are we part of groups? What are the rewards of belonging to groups?

What are some of the disadvantages of belonging to groups?

Religious Differences

Grades 2–6

Materials: phone books from various cities and smaller communities

Procedure:

1. Ask what churches, if any, the children attend. List these on the board.

2. Ask what other churches or religions there are. Add these to the list. Have students check phone books for the names of other churches.

🍎 Older students can research and make oral reports on the beliefs of the world's major religions.

Discussion:

What are some of the churches or religions you've heard of?

Are there any listed that you've never heard of?

Why are there so many different religions?

🍎 Stress that what each person believes and values is an individual choice that is right for that person.

Political Beliefs

Grades 3–6

Materials: newspaper accounts of elections, pictures of candidates

Procedure:

1. During election season, take students to visit polling places, if possible, and see a voting machine.

2. Bring in pictures of major candidates, and describe major issues. Have the class decide what makes a good candidate. What criteria would they use if they were voting?

3. Help the class understand the difference between making a decision by voting and by consensus (see chapter seven), and the difference between voting and public opinion polls.

Discussion:

What should all candidates have in common?

Why do people disagree about important issues?

When is coming to consensus a good way to make decisions?

What are some problems with it? (It's often slow.)

When is voting a good way to make decisions?

What are some problems with it? (It can leave the minority feeling left out or abused.)

Differences in Beliefs and Values

Grades K–6

Procedure:

1. Teach the children to vote thumbs up for *yes* or *agree*, arms folded for *indifferent* or *don't care*, and thumbs down for *disagree* or *no*.

2. Read a list of items such as the ones below, and have the children vote. Wait long enough between each item so that everyone can see how the class members have voted.

How many of you like spinach?

Can swim?

Think kids should watch all the TV they want?

Believe homework should be abolished?

3. Choose issues to suit the age level and sophistication of your students and the standards of the community in which you teach. Stress that what people believe and value is an individual choice that is right for them.

Discussion:

What are beliefs or values?

How do we acquire them?

Why are they important?

How can people who have differing values get along?

🍎 Values clarification strategies abound (see the Bibliography of Resources), and any public affirmation of values such as this will help children see that different people believe different things.

What's Ethnic?

Grades 2–6

Procedure:

1. Brainstorm a list of ethnic groups, and write it on the board.

2. Ask, "What traits make these groups similar to each other? Different?" Elicit answers that refer to homeland, language, customs, and appearance. From this information, develop a definition of *ethnic group*. Have students check this definition with the dictionary.

Discussion:

What ethnic background do you have?

Are we all from different ethnic backgrounds?

What are some of the cultural traditions of your group?

Ethnic Bulletin Boards

Grades K–6

Procedure:

Bulletin boards can be a wonderful means of exploring the benefits of diversity. You might try choosing an ethnic group each month and building a display on the topic of that group. Students can bring in artifacts or pictures to incorporate into the display.

Another approach I've found successful is to create weekly displays based on famous people and their contributions to society. One of my students once came up with a bulletin board quiz that contained such items as "What black woman helped slaves escape?" and "What Italian man invented the vacuum tube?" After the questions were actual strings that the students then attached to pictures of these people.

Ethnic Differences

Grades K–6

Procedure:

1. Have the children find out their ethnic ancestry. Locate countries of origin on a map or globe. Remind the class that, except for Native Americans, everyone came here in historical times from some other land.

2. There are many other activities one can base on multicultural themes. Build lessons around ethnic foods, crafts, clothing, literature, folk and fairy tales, or games. Older children can research the contributions of various ethnic groups. Stress that American culture has been enriched by the contributions of its many ethnic groups. Resources for multicultural education are listed in the Bibliography of Resources.

Copycats

Grades K–4

Procedure:

1. Choose a leader to stand before the class. Explain that he or she is the leader and that everyone should copy what he or she says or what he or she does.

2. Have the activity continue for at least five minutes. At first, the kids will giggle, but you want to move beyond fun to tedium. Then discuss.

Discussion:

How did it feel at first to be a copycat?

How did it feel after a while?

Why was it [boring, tedious, dreary]?

How did it feel for the leader to have everything copied?

What would it be like if everyone always did the same thing?

Zombie

Grades K–6

Materials: whistle

Procedure:

1. This is a game about conformity and the value of diversity. Explain to the class that they will all become zombies in a few minutes. As zombies, they must all do the same things, though not necessarily at the same time.

2. Have the class decide what five things a zombie can do. For example, zombies might be able to sit down, stand up, walk around the room stiff-legged, sharpen pencils, and erase the board. Whatever five things they can do, they cannot do anything else.

3. Explain that you will be the zombie patrol. If you see a zombie doing something zombies are not able to do, you will blow your whistle, and all zombies must freeze while you count to fifteen.

4. Play the game for ten to fifteen minutes, and then discuss.

Discussion:

What was it like at first being a zombie?

After a while, how did it feel always to do the same things?

How does diversity make life more interesting?

Class Gift, Part 1[6]

Grades K–3, (4, 5)

Materials: magic box (an empty box decorated as a present)

Procedure:

1. Hold up the magic box. Say, "Let's pretend I'm going shopping, and I'm going to buy a present for each boy and girl in this class."

2. Hand the box to one child. Say, "What present would you like? . . . Well, since I don't have time to get all kinds of different presents, I'm going to get *everyone* a ——."

3. Use this demonstration as the basis for a class discussion of the value of differences. With older students, use it also to introduce the concept of *generalizing*.

Discussion:

Would everyone be happy with that gift? Why not?

Why don't you all want the same thing?

How about getting everyone with black hair the same gift? What would be wrong with that?

Prejudice Activities

These lessons are designed to help students better understand cognitively the nature of generalizing, stereotyping, and prejudice. As I mentioned earlier, it is not enough for students to have experiences that counter stereotypes and prejudices they have. They also need to acquire an understanding of the processes involved. Those activities in chapter five having to do with perception and frame of reference are valuable additions here. For older pupils, excellent supplements to these are lesson in critical reading skills, propaganda detection, critical TV viewing skills, and so on.

Prejudice Discussion

Grades K–4, (5, 6)   **Materials:** dictionaries, *Green Eggs and Ham* by Dr. Seuss

Procedure:

1. Write the term *prejudice* on the board, and define it. Have older students look it up in the dictionary.

2. Read *Green Eggs and Ham* to younger students (kindergarten through fourth grade) as an example of one kind of prejudice. (Some fifth and sixth graders won't be offended by the book if you stress the fact that you are reading it for a purpose.)

Discussion:

What kinds of prejudice do you know about?

What kinds are fairly harmless?

What kinds are very harmful?

Whom do they harm?

Could prejudice be beneficial? (See Whom Do You Trust, later in this chapter.)

What might cause a prejudice to develop?

What's the difference between prejudice and dislike?

Tolerance Vocabulary

Grades 3–6

Procedure:

Vocabulary work provides a good means of assessing whether or not students have grasped cognitively the concepts related to tolerance.

1. Construct (or have students construct) crossword puzzles, word searches, scrambled word puzzles, and fill-in-the-blank puzzles.

2. Use tolerance vocabulary in spelling, writing, and alphabetizing assignments. Some tolerance vocabulary items are:

generalization	difference	segregation
prejudice	similarity	fear
discrimination	respect	status
scapegoat	tolerance	beliefs
ethnic	intolerance	values
stereotype	diversity	

Class Gift, Part 2

Grades K–4

Materials: two presents (one nicely wrapped, containing dirt or litter; the other shabbily wrapped, containing a nice present for the classroom)

Procedure:

1. Display the two gifts. Say, "These boxes contain gifts for the class. Let's vote on which gift you would like."

2. Open the box for which the majority voted (chances are, it will be the pretty box). Set the box aside and open the other present.

3. During the discussion, review the term *prejudice* and discuss kinds of prejudice. Relate prejudice to stereotyping and generalizing.

Discussion:

Why did you choose the box you did?

Did the appearance of the box have anything to do with its contents?

Does what a person looks like have anything to do with what he or she is like inside?

What did you learn from this experience?

Stress that appearance doesn't always indicate what someone is like. (Sometimes it does, of course.)

All Kids

Grades 3–6

Procedure:

1. Review the concept of generalizing. Ask the class to think about generalizations adults make about kids. Have them complete the sentence stub, "All kids ———."

2. On the board, make two tally charts, one headed *Positive* and *Negative* and the other headed *True* and *False*.

3. Have the students read their generalizations aloud. Have the class decide if each generalization is true or false, positive or negative.

4. Discuss the results, making sure the students understand that generalizing is not inherently bad, but that problems arise when generalizations aren't rooted in fact.

Discussion:

Why do people make generalizations?

How could generalizations be harmful?

How might they be helpful?

How might generalizations fuel conflict?

What could you do if you hear someone making an inaccurate generalization?

Stereotypes[7]

Grades K–6

Materials: pictures of modern Native Americans engaged in various occupations, crayons, paper

Procedure:

1. Have the children imagine that they are out west and suddenly see an Indian. Have them draw a picture of an Indian. Most of the children will draw Native Americans in traditional garb, probably with bows and arrows.

2. Display the photographs of modern Native Americans. Discuss with the children the differences between their drawings of Native Americans and the photographs.

3. Introduce the concept of stereotypes, i.e., generalizations about a group of people.

Discussion:

Where did you get your mental picture of Native Americans?

Are all Native Americans alike?

What might be some negative effects of the stereotypes we have of Native Americans?

Reinforce the children's understanding of the concept of stereotypes. Have the children describe how Japanese live or Africans live. They probably have stereotyped ideas about these people as well. Then show photographs that refute the stereotypes that emerge. If the topic was Africans, point out that there are many African countries and ways of life. Filmstrips available about life in other countries not only help dispel stereotypes but also provide a good starting point for discussion of cultural differences and similarities.

Male-Female Stereotypes

Grades K–6

Materials: magazines, scissors, paste, paper for mounting

Procedure:

Have students work in groups, cutting out pictures of men and women engaged in various activities. Then have them make two collages, one labeled *Men* and the other *Women*. Discuss the collages when complete.

Discussion:

What things are the men doing? The women?

Could a man do the things women are pictured doing? Vice versa?

What stereotypes are evident here?

How do magazines, TV, and other media support stereotypes?

How could they break down stereotypes instead of supporting them?

Stereotypes of Disabled People[8]

Grades (K–2), 3–6

Materials: pencils, paper

Procedure:

Discuss disabilities (see the physical differences—physical disabilities activity presented earlier in this chapter). Read the children the following questionnaire. Tally the answers.

What do you think?		yes	no	some-times
Can disabled kids:	wash dishes?	____	____	____
	cook?	____	____	____
	babysit?	____	____	____
	cut grass?	____	____	____
	cry?	____	____	____
	kiss parents goodnight?	____	____	____
	fight?	____	____	____
	play baseball?	____	____	____
	climb trees?	____	____	____
Can disabled adults:	cook dinner?	____	____	____
	wash dishes?	____	____	____
	change diapers?	____	____	____
	do laundry?	____	____	____
	have children?	____	____	____
	fix a broken window?	____	____	____
	drive?	____	____	____
	support a family?	____	____	____

(The answers should, of course, all be *sometimes*.)

Discussion:

What stereotypes do we have of disabled people?

Are all disabled people the same?

How does stereotyping hurt disabled people?

 You might try having the kids take this questionnaire home.

Stereotyping Buzz Words

Grades 3–6

Procedure:

1. Explain that some words are buzz words, signaling possible stereo-typing or overgeneralizing. Brainstorm a list of these words, such as all, most, none, every, any, everyone. If students have trouble getting the idea, give the following example: "All kids tell lies." Ask if it's true or if it's a stereotype. Ask, "What's the buzz word that makes this sentence a stereotyping one?"

2. Read aloud sentences similar to the examples below. When students hear buzz words they identified in the brainstorming, they should raise hands and shout, "Buzz!" Then finish the sentence, and have students decide whether the statement rests on a stereotype or over-generalization.

   All the kids in this school are smart.

   Most of my friends are cheerful.

   I'd ask black kids to my party, but none live near me.

   Most Jewish kids are smart.

Discussion:

How could overgeneralizing lead to prejudice?

Is an overgeneralization or a stereotype accurate?

Why are these words buzz words?

What are more accurate or fair words to use?

Stereotyped Attitudes

Grades 1–6

Procedure:

1. On the board, write "Girls," "Boys," and "Old people." Ask the children to tell you things girls can't do, things boys can't do, and things old people can't do.

2. The boys and girls will very quickly challenge the stereotypes about themselves. Use this to start discussion.

3. Ask the students if they know of any older people who refute the stereotypes mentioned about them.

Discussion:

Is it true that [girls, boys, old people] can't do this?

Is it fair to think so? Why not?

Why do some people think that way about [old people, boys, girls]?

Are there some boys who can't ———?

What are people doing when they say things like this?

What are some possible negative effects of this kind of stereotyped attitude?

Stereotypes and You[9]

Grades 4–6

Materials: pencils, paper

Procedure:

1. Have each student choose a group (for instance, ethnic, religious, or racial) to which he or she belongs.

2. Each student should label the top of a piece of paper with the name of his or her group. Then, for homework, have students ask their families to name five ways that people stereotype their group. Encourage them to include at least one positive stereotype.

3. Have the children return the papers to you. As this is likely to be a sensitive area, don't discuss the stereotypes of particular groups. Instead, discuss how it felt to *be* stereotyped.

Discussion:

What did it feel like when you heard some of the stereotypes?

Had you heard them before?

Are the stereotypes true? Do they describe you and your family?

What would some negative effects of the stereotypes, even the positive ones, be?

🍎 This activity can be controversial, so use your judgment. A letter home thoroughly explaining what you are doing and why helps. If in doubt, skip this activity.

Students' Stereotypes

Grades 4–6

Procedure:

1. On the board, write the following words (use your judgment):

teenager	cheerleader	city kid
politician	gay man	policeman
school principal	poor person	football player

2. Have the class tell words or phrases they associate with these groups.

Discussion:

How are you stereotyping here?

Are all the stereotypes negative?

Does anyone know a [*group member*] who is not [*stereotype*]?

How could a positive stereotype have a negative effect?

Name-calling

Grades 2–4

Materials: name-calling worksheet (see Appendix)

Procedure:

1. Have the children complete the name-calling worksheet, share their responses one item at a time, and discuss.

2. Emphasize that, at one time or another, everyone has called people names and has been called names. Stress empathizing with the victim and looking for more appropriate ways for the name-caller to express feelings.

3. Use the sheets for role playing, puppet shows, skit material, or whatever might interest your class.

Talking to Yourself

Grades 2–4, (5, 6)

Procedure:

1. Put the following flow chart on the board:

    1. What's going on?
        ↓
    2. What's the truth?
        ↓
    3. Why might they say this?
        ↓
    4. How do you feel?
        ↓
    5. What will you do?

    Explain that when someone puts you down, it helps to talk to yourself, following these steps in your mind. Walk the class through the flow chart with the following example:

    1. Barbara called me a fat liar.

    2. The truth is that I am a little heavy, but I'm not a liar. I told her the truth.

    3. She doesn't want to hear the truth right now. It upsets her, so she wants to upset me. She feels better putting me down.

    4. I feel a little hurt, but I'll survive. I know I'm truthful.

    5. I'll walk away and play with some other kids.

2. This activity works well with the problem puppets, too.

    🍎 This technique really does help young children learn to shrug off name-calling. Older children might benefit from it, too.

Discussion:

Why do some people put other people down?

Why might talking to yourself help you deal with put-downs?

What does it mean to let something roll off your back?

Greenskins

Grades 4–6

Procedure:

1. With the class, decide the characteristics of a new minority group called greenskins, or greenies. Discuss their employment, income, level of education, language patterns, and religious traditions.

2. Divide students into groups. Some groups are low-income, some middle-income, and some rich. Have the groups write down three ways they might discriminate against the greenies, and three ways they think they might benefit from practicing this discrimination. Have groups share their lists.

🍎 This activity requires a certain amount of maturity and sophistication on the part of your students. It is important that you discuss it thoroughly and that the students understand that any imagined benefits of discrimination are bound to turn out to be illusory.

Discussion:

Does putting the greenies down really enhance the status of other groups?

What do nongreenies lose by discriminating against greenies?

What are better ways for people to enhance their self-esteem?

I Had a Bad Experience[10]

Grades 2–6

Procedure:

1. Tell the children that prejudice often begins with a single bad experience that gets generalized and fed into a stereotype.

2. Have the children think of a person who is different from themselves—the difference need not be racial or ethnic—with whom they had a bad experience. Ask volunteers to tell about some of these experiences.

3. If students have difficulty, ask if they have ever had a bad experience with:

> a dentist
>
> a bus driver
>
> a teacher
>
> a black kid
>
> a lesbian
>
> a football player
>
> a police officer
>
> a big kid
>
> an Asian-American kid

(The choices are up to you.) Ask for volunteers to tell about the experience.

Discussion:

Did your bad experience develop into a prejudice? Why or why not?

How could it have developed into a prejudice?

What could you do if you felt yourself developing a prejudice?

What can you do if other people are prejudiced?

Fear of the Unknown

Grades 2–6

Materials: three-by-five-inch index cards, pencils, box labeled *Unknown*

Procedure:

1. Distribute three-by-five cards. Have students anonymously describe on the cards something they don't know much about that consequently frightens them. Have them drop the cards in the box.

2. Read the cards aloud. Discuss.

Discussion:

Which of these are scary even when you know more about them?

Why do unknown things provoke fear?

What can you do to overcome such fear?

Are there groups of people you don't know much about?

Are they scary as a result?

What could you do about that?

Intergroup Meeting[11]

Grades 4–6

Materials: large paper, markers

Procedure:
When a class becomes polarized (even to a slight degree), this technique for examining perceptions is enlightening.

1. Present the class with the names of two groups, and have them identify the group to which they belong. Students who do not belong can be observers.

2. Give each group markers and paper. Have each group make up the following lists, without communicating with the other group:

list 1: characteristics the members think describe their group, i.e., how they perceive themselves

list 2: characteristics they think the other group would say they have

list 3: characteristics they think describe the other group

3. Have each group read its first list, then its second, and finally its third, all without comment or discussion.

4. Have the groups meet by themselves to discuss:

How was your image of the other group different from the other group's perception of itself?

Adapted by permission of A&W Publishers, Inc. from *Developing Effective Classroom Groups* by Gene Stanford. Copyright © 1977, Hart Publishing Company, Inc.

What behavior on the part of the other group's members would lead to this difference in perception?

What have they done to make you see them so differently from the way they see themselves?

5. Mix group members up in a circle and discuss ways to reduce misconceptions and misunderstandings.

Three Exceptions

Grades 2-6

Procedure:

This simple trick was shared with me by a sixty-year-old teacher who attended one of my workshops. She had learned it from her own fifth grade teacher, who told her students that whenever they caught themselves thinking a prejudiced or stereotyped thought about an individual or group, they should try to think of three exceptions to the prejudice or stereotype. My acquaintance said that the habit of doing this had stayed with her for fifty years, and so she felt it was worth passing on to others.

Prejudices and Dislikes

Grades 2-6

Materials: prejudices and dislikes worksheet (see Appendix)

Procedure:

1. Review the definition of prejudice. Ask, "How is a prejudice different from a dislike?"

2. Read the story below, and ask students to characterize the attitudes of Janet and Alice as either dislike or prejudice.

    Janet is a disabled girl—she has a brace on her leg and uses a wheelchair. She is white. She is always pushing Alice down. Alice is a black girl. Alice does not like Janet because Janet always rams Alice with her wheelchair. Janet doesn't like Alice because Janet believes that black people are always stealing.

3. Distribute the worksheet for students to complete. Discuss responses.

Discussion:

Which items were dislikes? Which were prejudices?

What makes them dislikes? Prejudices?

How could dislikes become prejudices?

Revealing Statements

Grades 4-6

Procedure:

1. Place the following sentences on the board:

    It would be better if teachers were stricter.

    It's a shame when a mother has to work outside the home.

    There's only one right way to do things.

Everyone has a right to be happy.

People will try to get you if they can.

Violence is part of human nature and will never change.

Everything that happens to us is preordained.

2. Divide students into groups. Have them discuss the statements for fifteen minutes, and decide what each statement reveals about the speaker and whether or not it has anything to do with prejudice. Groups should choose a notetaker who will keep track of the group's conclusions and report to the class.

🍎 During the discussion, it is important to stress that, although some of the attitudes revealed by these statements might not be inconsistent with prejudice, it is not fair to judge people as prejudiced on the basis of a few statements. During the discussion, however, point out that an inflexible, untrusting outlook is likely to lead to prejudice, and discuss why.

Discussion:

Which of these statements reflects a prejudice?

Which reveals an inflexible or intolerant attitude?

How might such attitudes lead to prejudice?

Is it fair to judge people on the basis of one or two statements?

Whom Do You Trust?

Grades K–6   **Procedure:**

1. In groups of five or six, have the students do a trust fall: the group forms a circle around one member, who closes eyes, falls in any direction, and is supported by the group. Repeat so that everyone gets an opportunity to be in the center.

2. Apropos of this activity, discuss trust and trustworthiness.

3. Discuss strangers, and emphasize being very cautious around them. With older students, develop a trustworthiness checklist of things to consider before trusting an unknown person.

Discussion:

Why shouldn't you talk to strangers?

Does that mean all strangers are bad?

How would you get to trust them?

What do you look for in a new person to decide if you can trust him or her?

Why is trust important in our classroom?

What could you do to show that you are trustworthy?

Discrimination Games

Grades 3–6   **Procedure:**

1. Introduce the term *discrimination*, which means, in this context, exclusion of people based on the prejudices of the excluder.

2. Introduce a discrimination game by explaining what the group criteria are, which group is the excluder, and how the exclusion will work. For example:

   1. Have eight to ten students form a tight circle and lock arms. Another student has one minute to break into the circle. If he or she does, then the group has a new member. Give everyone a turn being the outsider. Ask, "How does it feel to be a member of the ingroup? How does it feel to be left out? When you tried to get into the group and failed, how did that feel?"

   2. Divide students into groups on the basis of some criterion—hair color or eye color, sex, or something artificial such as blue arm bands. Arbitrarily designate one group as superior. The superior group gets special privileges; the inferior group is denied privileges. Ask, "How does it feel to be considered superior? How does it feel to be considered inferior?"

Discussion:

Have any of you ever been discriminated against? What happened? What did you do?

How do prejudice and discrimination affect conflict?

🍎 Use discrimination games with discretion. Because they provoke such emotion and anxiety, you should weigh carefully the maturity of your students, the standards of your community, and whether or not you feel fully prepared carefully to help the kids understand the experience.

Critical Incidents

Grades K–6

Procedure:

The critical incidents technique is good for starting discussions about some of the issues in this chapter. Here are some examples:

1. *Name-calling.* James is a new boy at school and is just beginning to make friends. The group of boys he's getting to be friends with are always calling people names, such as nigger, wop, faggot, and so on. James doesn't like to hear people called these names, but he doesn't want to lose his new friends.

   What's the problem?

   What could James do?

   Have you ever had a similar problem?

   What did you do?

   What would you do if you were James?

2. *Scapegoating.* Ming is the only Asian-American student in the class. Lately there has been an epidemic of stealing from people's desks— lunch money, small toys, and pencils. Many kids have started to say that Ming did it, even though they have no evidence.

What's the problem?

If you were in that class, what would you do?

What is scapegoating?

Why would the class scapegoat Ming?

3. *Discrimination.* Paula, Jean, Katherine, and Mary Frances are close friends and have formed a sort of club. They've decided to let Gail in because they like her, but not Carmelita, because she is Puerto Rican. Katherine and Gail think this is wrong, but Paula, Jean, and Mary Frances are firm.

What's the problem?

What should Gail and Katherine do?

What is a clique?

What is what the girls are doing called?

How does discriminating hurt the clique?

Have you ever been in a similar situation?

Notes

1. Louise Fitzhugh, *Harriet the Spy* (New York: Harper and Row, 1964), p. 277. Used with permission.

2. A good summary of research in this area is Jean D. Grambs, *Understanding Intergroup Relations* (National Education Association, 1973).

3. David A. Shiman, *The Prejudice Book* (New York: Anti-Defamation League of B'nai B'rith, 1979), p. 9.

4. Joe Abruscato and Jack Hassard, *The Earth People Activity Book* (Glenview, Ill.: Scott, Foresman, 1978), pp. 20–21. Adapted with permission.

5. Both physical differences activities were suggested by Suzanne Tonner.

6. I learned the class gift activities from Will James.

7. Suggested by Ted Sicker.

8. Ellen Barnes et al., *What's the Difference?* (Syracuse, N.Y.: Human Policy Press, 1978), pp. 62–63. Used with permission.

9. Shiman, *The Prejudice Book*, p. 83. Used with permission.

10. Ibid, p. 111. Used with permission.

11. Adapted by permission of A&W Publishers, Inc. from *Developing Effective Classroom Groups* by Gene Stanford. Copyright© 1977, Hart Publishing Co., Inc.

Chapter 9

Handling Conflicts with Parents, Other Teachers, and Administrators

I love teaching. I love the kids.
It's everybody else I can't stand.

—*overheard at a teacher's convention*

I would guess that at one time or another each of us has felt like that unknown teacher quoted above. Conflicts with children are not the only ones you encounter in this job. You must also deal with parents, with other teachers, and with administrators. In the course of these dealings, conflicts arise.

These are important conflicts, and they must be handled with skill and tact. It has been my experience that the principles of creative conflict resolution are as useful in these conflicts as in the ones that occur in your classroom.

Conflicts with Parents

Teachers seem to agree that parents' attitudes toward teachers have changed. Changed for the worse. No longer can you count on a parent to

179

support you or even necessarily to respect you. It sometimes seems as though a parent is as likely to sue you as back you up. So, many teachers wish for the good old days when they had automatic parental respect. Other teachers look for places to lay blame when they come into conflict with parents.

Both of these exercises, although understandable, are counterproductive. In the first place, the good old days, if they ever existed, are gone; longing for them won't bring them back. In the second place, unquestioning parental support of teachers is not necessarily a good thing. In a healthy society, people should question authority, including the authority of educators. There are, of course, constructive and destructive ways to do this, and I'm not denying the fact that parents can on occasion behave irrationally or reprehensibly. But parent vs. teacher conflicts, like any other conflicts, can be handled functionally, to the benefit of all.

Causes of Parent vs. Teacher Conflicts

Parent vs. teacher conflicts are rooted in causes I have outlined in other contexts. For example, poor communication can lead to misunderstandings about what is going on in school, and why. If there is no spirit of cooperation, problems can get sidestepped as the parties focus on personalities rather than on working together to solve the problem at hand. Intolerance can lead to conflicts of values, goals, and attitudes, usually concerning what is important to learn and why. Power struggles can develop over the question of what's important in school and who will wield the most influence in the situation.

Whatever their cause, parent vs. teacher conflicts are complicated by three factors:

1. Parents and teachers have a limited number of contacts during the year. The contacts they do have seem very important as a result, perhaps more important than they are.

2. Many parents have bad mental associations with school, because of either their own schooling or their prior school contacts as parents. They bring this negative frame of reference to any parent-teacher encounter.

3. Roles are changing, and the question of who is responsible for what aspects of the child's life is no longer clear. Parents and teachers can suspect each other of demanding too much or claiming too much authority.

Improving Relationships with Parents

As you know, an ounce of prevention . . . . Any attempt you make to improve communication, cooperation, and tolerance and downplay the power aspects of the relationship should improve your dealings with parents.

Don't assume that kids are conveying accurately (or at all) information about what is going on at school. Send home letters periodically that explain what you are doing, and why. Anticipate questions in advance, and have solid justifications for what you're doing. Stress the academic benefits of a project or program. Send home positive notes concerning work and behavior, not just negative ones. Try to send home a personal note to each child's parents every month. If one month you must send a negative note, send a positive note as soon as possible. These are obvious but often neglected preventive measures.

Increase the number of positive contacts you have with parents any way you can. Parents are rich in skills, information, and experience. Use them. Don't be afraid of having parents in your room. You're a nice person, and you're doing a good job. Take every opportunity to demonstrate your concern for the child, not your concern for maintaining your program or philosophy. Solicit parents' information and opinions about their children. Welcoming suggestions is a way to keep parental input from becoming strident.

Some parents have ideas that are very different from yours about children, school, and indeed life. Don't fall into the trap of condemning these differences, even silently. Such an attitude would be reflected in the way you interact with the parents and the child. Differences can be enriching; for this reason and for the sake of smooth relations, you should make every effort to accommodate them.

Approaching Parent vs. Teacher Conflicts

1. Don't assume anything. Stay calm and nondefensive, and don't leap to conclusions.

2. Let the parent talk as much as he or she wants. This may mean that you get to hear about a lot of anger and other emotion. Listen reflectively, and try to define the problem in nonjudgmental terms.

3. Put yourself in the parent's place as you listen. Bend over backward to understand his or her point of view.

4. Be prepared. Have at hand whatever documentation you may need, and be ready to discuss the problem in a calm, descriptive way.

5. Be sure you understand the parent's expectations in the situation, and that he or she understands yours.

6. Have assistance ready if appropriate. If you're discussing a difficult child, perhaps another teacher might offer her or his perspective. If you are discussing retention, perhaps a guidance counselor can also be present.

7. Don't make promises you can't keep. For example, you may think Edward should be retained, but you can't guarantee that doing so will ensure his success—or that not doing so will ensure his failure.

8. Know the limits. No matter how much you care about a student, you don't bear the final responsibility for raising him or her. It's not your place to try to do so. (I'm not speaking here, of course, of actual abuse —physical or emotional—or of neglect. If you suspect any of these, you have a legal obligation to contact the appropriate authorities.) If

all your efforts at persuasion fail, accept that fact gracefully, and focus on the new problem: "Where do we go from here?"

Negotiating with Parents

1. Define the problem. In doing so, touch on these questions: What are the parent's desires and expectations? What are yours? What are the areas of disagreement? Finally, is there common ground?

2. With the parent, list some possible courses of action; try to come up with at least two. Encourage the parent to defer judgment until you've both thought of all possible solutions.

3. Decide one on which you can agree. Should it be modified? How will you implement it?

4. Establish a follow-up procedure for reporting progress to the parent, and set a date for the first report.

5. If negotiations prove fruitless, suggest a delay. Say something like, "We've both got a lot to think about here. Why don't I call you tomorrow afternoon, and we can talk some more?" Or you might suggest a third party to help work things out, perhaps a social worker or guidance person you both trust.

Consider the following example. Mrs. Woodward believes that her daughter Kathleen is gifted but is not being challenged in Betty Alexander's fifth grade class. Betty is not convinced that Kathleen is gifted and has said so to Mrs. Woodward. Mrs. Woodward has just accused Betty of being an uninterested and ineffective teacher.

Mrs. W: Kathleen deserves all the opportunities you can give her to help her reach her potential.

BA: All my children deserve such opportunities, and I try to provide them. What I'm not sure of here is what you want me to do.

Mrs. W: I want you to give her challenging material.

BA: How, exactly? What kind of challenging material?

Mrs. W: Well, for one thing, I think we should think about having her skip a grade to sixth.

BA: We certainly can consider that. Anything else?

Mrs. W: I don't know. She's just not using her potential.

BA: She is already in an accelerated reading program, and is in the top math group. She performs in these groups, but she doesn't seem to be terribly excited by them.

Mrs. W: If you made them more interesting, she might.

BA: What interests her?

Mrs. W: She doesn't really get excited about much. She's not that type. She mostly likes to play with other kids.

BA: Based on what I see in class, I'd agree. She doesn't like to stand out, and I think that's a reason she is perhaps holding herself back.

Mrs. W: Well, I hadn't thought of that.

BA: You know, I think that a large part of the problem here is really how to motivate Kathleen to use some of her gifts. Would you agree? [*Mrs. Woodward nods.*] We could try developing some sort of special project, and give her a chance to be in on the planning. That way we would know she was interested.

Mrs. W: Maybe something with art. She likes art, even though that's not very academic.

BA: No, but maybe we could work something out with the art teacher and give the project an academic focus.

Mrs. W: I think she might like that, but it should probably involve other kids. Friends of hers.

BA: I think so, too. Why don't I talk with Mr. Abrams, the art teacher, and with Kathleen, and see what we come up with? I can get back to you in, say, three days to tell you what we've planned.

Mrs. W: What if that doesn't work?

BA: Then we'll just try something else. Now that we know we both have the same concern for Kathleen, I'm sure we'll make progress.

A parent's concern for a child can sometimes be expressed as anger toward the teacher. In any parent vs. teacher conflict, someone has to keep a cool head, and the responsibility is yours.

By staying nondefensive and showing her concern, Betty effectively disproved Mrs. Woodward's charge of lack of concern without ever directly addressing it. Betty patiently helped Mrs. Woodward clarify her rather vague charges and expectations in a way that took the attention off Betty and put it on the problem. By simply acknowledging (but not pursuing) skipping a grade as an option, Betty left it by the wayside as more useful and realistic ideas came up. Finally, notice how Betty not only thanked Mrs. Woodward, but also emphasized an optimistic and cooperative approach to the problem in the future.

Conflicts with Other Teachers

Conflicts with colleagues can be among the most troubling conflicts a teacher can face. It's very unpleasant to be on the outs with the people with whom you work. Teacher vs. teacher conflicts are like any other in that they can be classified as conflicts of resources, needs, or values. But in some ways it's more useful to classify them as personal or professional.

Professional conflicts are centered on your students or your teaching. Personal conflicts are centered on you.

Professional conflicts most often arise when teachers dispute who is responsible for children in a particular time and place ("Your children were running in the hall again") or when one teacher overtly or covertly questions another's competence ("None of her students has very legible handwriting"). A third source of professional conflict is professional jealousy, which arises when one teacher resents the activities or accomplishments of another.

Personal conflicts arise for all the reasons they arise in any context. Sometimes personal and professional conflicts mix; when they do, it is usually fairly easy to delineate the two types. This discussion concerns primarily professional conflicts and ways to prevent them.

Improving Relationships with Other Teachers

Think of your school as a community. To make it a more caring community, you can apply the principles of the peaceable classroom to improve communication, cooperation, and tolerance.

Get to know the rest of the staff and, as with parents, try to establish a history of short, positive encounters. Offer to exchange ideas on teaching methods when it seems appropriate, but watch your step; teachers can be territorial with respect to their own classroom practice.

Try to get clear policy established about who is responsible for students when they are in the halls, bathrooms, cafeteria, and other common areas. Since other teachers in the building are likely to encounter your students from time to time, you can usefully distribute suggestions for dealing with particularly difficult children from your class. When a problem does arise, encourage everyone to focus on the problem, not the teachers or children involved. Try to get problems resolved as quickly as possible, before they escalate.

Be careful in the teachers' room, where tolerance and intolerance are most clearly revealed. Set strict standards for yourself concerning what you will and will not discuss in the teachers' room. If you ask for help, do so in a way that will encourage constructive suggestions, not negative or hopeless remarks. Keep your strongest opinions to yourself unless they generate light, not heat.

Approaching Teacher vs. Teacher Conflicts

1. Remember, you can't please everybody.

2. Define the conflict. Who's involved? What's causing the problem? Where did it start? How might it end if you ignore it?

3. Ask yourself: What is this relationship worth to you? Is the conflict interfering with your teaching or with school morale? What kind of risk are you willing to take for this conflict? Let the answers determine the extent to which you will attempt reconciliation. Sometimes the effort is just not worth the probable cost; sometimes it's worth a great deal personally or professionally.

4. Once you've weighed the risk and value of trying to resolve the conflict, decide your strategy:

> Ignore it.
>
> Work through another person.
>
> Use a conflict resolution technique.
>
> Confront it angrily.
>
> Ignore it, but plot revenge.

(The last two aren't recommended, needless to say.)

5. Know who your friends are. You might need them for support or intervention, or to help you keep proper perspective.

Resolving Teacher vs. Teacher Conflicts

Many of the techniques described in chapters two and three will work in teacher vs. teacher conflicts. The problem is often how to suggest such an approach. This is not too difficult at a faculty meeting where everyone is trying to establish policy concerning a particular issue, but it can be thorny in a conflict with a teacher or group of teachers in a less formal context. A trusted intermediary is most helpful in this latter case.

Conflicts with Administrators

Contrary to what sometimes seems to be popular faculty opinion, teachers and administrators do not usually conflict because administrators are vindictive and irrational. To really understand teacher-administrator conflicts, you must understand how administrators think. Most administrators are concerned with:

1. the quality of education their schools give
2. the educational, emotional, and social needs of the children in their care
3. the public image of their schools
4. the happiness of their teachers
5. budgets

Teachers and administrators tend to conflict over needs and values, specifically as they relate to the five factors above. So, to reduce teacher vs. administrator conflicts, it helps to address yourself to the above-mentioned factors.

Improving Relationships with Administrators

To improve relations with, for instance, the principal of your school, establish a history of casual, positive contacts. Display a friendly and sincere interest in his or her personal life.

Offer help. Serve on committees and demonstrate your concern for a positive school community.

Do your job, and do it well. Show the principal positive notes you get from parents. Make sure he or she knows the exciting things you are doing. If appropriate, get publicity such as newspaper coverage for your efforts. (I know of two teachers who actually saved their jobs by the judicious use of publicity.)

Approaching Teacher vs. Administrator Conflicts

1. Recognize and take into account the power dynamic at work in your relationship. You are now in the position with respect to the administrator that your students are in with you. Be tactful. Learn how best to approach the administrator; try to discover and keep in mind what he or she finds offensive, trivial, and important.

2. Listen. Try to understand his or her concerns and expectations. Put yourself in his or her position, and try to come up with a definition of the problem that you can both accept.

3. Be prepared to back up your statements, requests, programs, or complaints with evidence, but try not to put him or her on the defensive. Evidence presented in mountainous quantity or with expression of anger will only make the administrator dig in his or her heels.

4. Once again, know who your allies are. Don't go over the administrator's head, but ask yourself if there is someone to whom you can talk about the situation. Perhaps that person can help you sort it out. Is there someone who might intercede on your behalf? (Remember, complaining in the teachers' room is not likely to improve things.)

5. You must know the line beyond which you will either give in gracefully or take your dispute elsewhere (to your union's grievance committee, for example).

Some teachers' associations have established mediation boards to help work out teacher vs. administrator or teacher vs. teacher disputes. Let's encourage more of these in the future so that we can stop suffering from conflict and start benefiting from it.

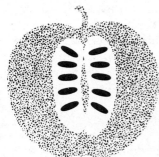

Chapter 10

Putting It All in Practice

One day I was helping a student with long division, something that gave him a great deal of trouble. In the course of working with him, I kept asking, "Do you understand?" Finally, he looked at me in exasperation and said, "Mr. Kreidler, my problem isn't understanding; my problem is *doing it*!"

In the course of reading this book and working with the material, you have probably had questions about how to put creative conflict resolution into actual practice, and I'll try to address those questions here. First, I have one general piece of advice. Creative conflict resolution is a serious subject, but don't be somber as you practice its techniques. I hope that the approach will be as much fun for you and your students as it has been for me. If you maintain a sense of excitement and experimentation (for this is how the techniques were developed), you will not only enjoy the process itself more, you are likely to find yourself involved in your teaching in a way you weren't before.

The following are the questions I am most frequently asked at workshops and speaking engagements, and my answers.

Q: I think all this is very exciting, but where do you find time to do it?

A: My school system, like many others, requires that a certain number of minutes per week be spent on reading, math, and so on. Since very little time is left for anything else, I have been forced to integrate creative conflict resolution with the rest of the curriculum. I still reserve time Tuesday and Thursday afternoons for special projects, and often the projects relate to conflict resolution. I also take advantage of teachable moments as they arise.

Q: What is your time line for the year?

A: When school begins in September, I start introducing those aspects of the program that are most immediate: Effective Rules, establishing such procedures as helping each other with work, and beginning community-building activities such as cooperative games. For most of September, I focus on community building by using more cooperative games and get-acquainted activities. I also use conflict resolution techniques to deal with any conflicts that arise.

In late September I introduce cooperative activities. First I use non-content-oriented activities. About mid-October, I add activities related to subject matter. Also in October, I begin to pay close attention to communication skills, and I continue to do so into November.

During November and December, I focus on tolerance. In January, I begin taking a serious look at the nature of conflict and teaching the kids to be peacemakers. In February, I begin working on negative feelings.

Sprinkled throughout the year are activities focused on feelings (in a broad sense), conflict resolution techniques (as the need arises), cooperative games, community building, and appreciation of differences. My time line changes from year to year, and your time line may look completely different.

Q: You talk about integrating the approach. How do you do it?

A: Some of the creative conflict resolution program is integrated as routine classroom management procedure. Other aspects fit very well into standard subject areas.

Communication skills can, of course, be covered in language arts. I've also found that communication activities fit in very well with work on science, social studies, and health. Cooperation skills, once learned, can be used in any subject area, including physical education. Emotions can be discussed in conjunction with language arts, reading, art, social studies, and health. Conflict is often a topic appropriate to the same subjects. Creativity and problem solving, which are related to conflict resolution, can be developed in these areas as well as in science and math.

Discussion of and appreciation for individual differences can be fostered in any subject area. Cultural differences can be discussed in conjunction with reading, language arts, art, and social studies.

I try to emphasize good communication practices every day. I also try to include an emotional awareness activity every day, and I daily try to mention some positive aspect of diversity. Finally, I include at least one cooperative activity per day, even if it's only a game.

Q: How do parents react to all this?

A: I have never had a parent object to the creative conflict resolution approach. I simply tell them at the beginning of the year that I try to help the children learn to work together and settle disputes peaceably. Often they are very supportive—after all, what parent wouldn't like a little less squabbling around the house?

There's nothing particularly controversial about the program. It does not try to teach students to be pacifists, which is something many parents would find objectionable. Violence and fighting are not ruled out as responses to conflict, just discouraged. Neither are children taught to be passive in the face of conflict. Just the opposite, in fact.

Several parents have told me how impressed they are with the way their children now confront and systematically try to solve problems they encounter.

Q: Can the creative conflict resolution approach be applied to the entire school?

A: Certainly it can. Many schools have had success in making conflict resolution a schoolwide focus. As you might imagine, doing so can greatly enhance the effectiveness of such an approach.

I do have one caution, however. Unlike the so-called teacher-proof curricula, this program trusts teachers to make the important decisions of what gets taught, when it's taught, and how it's taught. This not only means a certain amount of increased work for teachers, it also means they must, to some degree, be committed to the program and care about whether or not it works. It should not—and probably, realistically speaking, cannot—be forced on anyone.

Q: I'm finding that some of the activities you suggest seem inappropriate to my class's maturity level and interests.

A: I've tried to give you material to cover many needs and topics. It's unlikely that you will use every lesson and suggested technique. I don't myself. Use them to meet your needs and the needs of your students. Change these lessons as necessary. Add to them; develop new ones, whatever you need. And while you're at it, write and let me know what you tried and how it worked. Anything any one of us can do to make the world a little less violent is important.

Q: What about guns and war toys in the classroom?

A: I don't have an easy answer to this one. Many people fear that such toys encourage acceptance of war and violence as ways to settle disputes. On the other hand, some say that violence is a fact of life in our society and that one way children can come to terms with it is through playing at it. There are studies that show that, when such toys are banned, children simply pretend their fingers are guns and lie when confronted, denying that they are playing at war games. In other words, at this point we simply aren't sure of the effect, if any, of such play.

I do not allow war toys inside my own classroom, and by providing compelling alternatives, I've found that the children do not in fact play at such games. I also ask the children not to play war games at recess, nor to draw war pictures, and I tell them why. Then, if they choose to do so (and some do), I accept it.

I don't worry about this too much, and I don't think you should, either. When I was a boy, I loved playing with toy guns, soldiers, cowboys, all of it. I changed. Ultimately, children must decide for themselves to pursue nonviolence. It can't be forced on them.

Q: How do you evaluate students' progress?

A: I use two methods, primarily. First, I observe carefully to see if the kids are indeed learning and using the skills of cooperation and communication in day-to-day interactions. I also observe their progress in positive emotional expression, tolerance, and, of course, creative responses to conflict. I try, by the way, to avoid the temptation to see only what I want to see.

I also give periodic tests, either written or oral, based on critical incidents (see chapter eight), to see if the children can in fact define conflicts, state both sides, develop solutions, and say how they might act in a particular situation. The limitation of this technique is that children are very good at telling you what you want to hear. The child who scores well on a test may never apply the skills.

On the whole, I find that these two approaches complement each other well and give me a pretty good idea not only of where the children are but also of where we need to go next.

Q: Can peaceable classroom concepts be extended beyond the classroom?

A: Absolutely. Particularly with older children, you can begin to apply the principles to conflicts in the larger community, the country, and even the world. Once the students have worked with the elements of the program in the classroom, they find it a particularly meaningful approach to current events. It's all part of peace education in general.

Q: What is peace education, exactly?

A: I see creative conflict resolution as belonging less to the field of classroom management or affective education than to the relatively new subject called peace education. This subject has three major components: increasing skills and awareness of conflict resolution, my special interest; multicultural education, i.e., learning about the people of the world with whom we share the planet; and the study of war, peace, and justice in the world, with an emphasis on preventing war and promoting peace and justice.

General Omar Bradley once wrote, "We know more about war than we know about peace, more about killing than we know about living. This is our twentieth-century claim to distinction and progress." Many people from all walks of life are realizing that we have learned too well the ways of violence and now need to learn the ways of peace.

Q: Wait a minute. That's all well and good, but my students live in a tough inner city environment, and they need to learn to defend themselves. I wouldn't be doing them any favor by teaching them the ways of peace.

A: First of all, let me say that I began developing this approach when I was working in tough, inner city classrooms. It was there that I realized the extent to which kids get locked into the aggression-passivity mentality. Indeed, I saw that, that even when it was clearly in a student's best interests not to fight, he or she still fought.

Your students and mine will learn to fight no matter what we do or don't do. As I've said before, this program does not rule out violence, except in the classroom and on school grounds. Instead, it presents what are often more effective alternatives to violence. You are not doing your students any favor by pretending that violence is the only option available to them.

Q: What can I expect from doing all this?

A: No curriculum is guaranteed. You are not, after all, the only influence on the children's lives. Kids learn all the time how to handle conflicts. They learn from parents, peers, community standards, and television. Needless to say, many of these are sending messages different from yours. There have been times, frankly, when I despaired of ever making a difference. But I stayed with it because I found it to be challenging and fun—and it always paid off eventually.

You should see growth—rapid in some cases, slow in others. There is no magic moment when students are suddenly able creatively to resolve all their conflicts. There will probably be no overnight successes, but there may well be some dramatic ones.

It is a wonderful experience for a teacher to watch a class of children grow over time into a caring community, able to work together, be tolerant and affirming of one another, and choose to approach conflict in ways they never did before. I have seen this happen year after year. So have teachers I know.

You might also see some surprising peacemaking talent emerge—from some very unlikely sources. But keep in mind that peacemaking is learned behavior, and all children have some talent for it. They, and this world they will inherit, deserve the chance to have it nurtured.

Thank you for reading this book. I would like to hear about your reactions to it and about your experiences with the program in your own classroom. I welcome your questions and suggestions. Also, please let me know if you would like information about workshops. You can contact me through the publisher. Good luck with *your* creative conflict resolution.

William J. Kreidler

Appendix

Worksheets and Game Cards

Name _____

Fight Form

With whom did you fight? _____

What was the problem? _____

_____

Why did you start fighting? (Give two reasons.) _____

_____

_____

Why did the other person fight with you? _____

_____

_____

Did fighting solve the problem? _____

What are three things you might try if this happens again?

1. _____

2. _____

3. _____

Is there anything you would like to say to the person you fought with? _____

_____

_____

From _Creative Conflict Resolution_, copyright © 1984 William J. Kreidler, published by Scott, Foresman and Company.

Worksheet in Upgrading Behavior

1. Begin by identifying the behavior pattern that needs to be changed.

    _____

2. Write down exactly what you saw yourself doing. I just _____

    _____.

3. When I'm in this kind of situation, this ____ is ____ is not what I usually do.
    My pattern is to _____
    when _____

4. My pattern gets me _____.
    Because of my pattern, I can _____,
    and I don't have to _____.
    My pattern helps me _____

    _____.

5. However, because of my pattern, I don't get to _____

    _____.
    My pattern costs me _____.
    I have to give up _____

    _____.

6. It feels to me as if my pattern:

    ____ gets me more than it costs me.

    ____ costs me more than it gets me.

    Therefore, I ____ do ____ do not want to change.

7. Instead of _____ as I've been doing, I think that
    _____ would be more satisfying to me. Something
    I could try next time _____
    would be to _____

    _____.

From *Creative Conflict Resolution*, copyright © 1984 William J. Kreidler, published by Scott, Foresman and Company.

Name _____

How I Respond to Conflicts

Fill in the appropriate circle for things you always, sometimes, or never do.

	Always	Sometimes	Never
When there's a conflict, I try to:			
1. hit the other person	◯	◯	◯
2. run away	◯	◯	◯
3. get help from another kid	◯	◯	◯
4. talk it out	◯	◯	◯
5. ignore it	◯	◯	◯
6. understand the other point of view	◯	◯	◯
7. make a joke of it	◯	◯	◯
8. get help from a grown-up	◯	◯	◯
9. make the other kid apologize	◯	◯	◯
10. apologize myself	◯	◯	◯
11. find out what the problem is	◯	◯	◯
12. listen to the other kid	◯	◯	◯
13. tell the kid to leave me alone	◯	◯	◯
14. say swear words	◯	◯	◯
15. get friends to gang up on the other kid	◯	◯	◯

From *Creative Conflict Resolution*, copyright © 1984 William J. Kreidler,
published by Scott, Foresman and Company.

First Steps

1. You want to cut up a birthday cake so it's fair. The first step you'd take is _____
    _____ .

2. You and your friends want to build a tree house. You have all the plans; the first step
    you'd take is _____
    _____ .

3. You want to buy a present for your friend. Your first step is _____
    _____ .

4. Ruth wants the boys to include her in baseball games. Her plan is to show what a good
    hitter she is. Her first step might be _____
    _____ .

5. Abe's grandmother lives with him and won't let him watch TV shows he likes. He
    wants to change her mind. His first step might be _____
    _____ .

From *Creative Conflict Resolution*, copyright © 1984 William J. Kreidler,
published by Scott, Foresman and Company.

Name _____

This Is How . . .

1. Your neighbor plays loud music at night. What could you do? _____

   _____

   How would you begin? _____

   What are two things that might happen? _____

   _____

2. The kid next to you copies off you. What could you do? _____

   _____

   How would you begin? _____

   What are two things that might happen? _____

   _____

3. A kid you know calls you names. What could you do? _____

   _____

   How would you begin? _____

   What are two things that might happen? _____

   _____

4. The water supply in your country is being poisoned by the pesticides used by the
   neighboring country. How would you solve this problem? _____

   _____

   How would you begin? _____

   What are two things that might happen? _____

   _____

5. Your planet has no weapons of any kind. You are being threatened by a neighboring
   planet that wants to take over and make your people slaves. What could you do?

   _____

   How would you begin? _____

   What are two things that might happen? _____

   _____

From *Creative Conflict Resolution*, copyright © 1984 William J. Kreidler, published by Scott, Foresman and Company.

Good Listener Checklist

When you are listening, do you:

1. look at the person speaking? _____ Yes _____ No
2. talk to other kids? _____ Yes _____ No
3. think about what the speaker is saying? _____ Yes _____ No
4. think about what you'll do later? _____ Yes _____ No
5. ask questions if you don't understand? _____ Yes _____ No
6. repeat what the speaker says to make sure you've got it right? _____ Yes _____ No

Write down three ways you will try to improve your listening:

1. _____
2. _____
3. _____

From *Creative Conflict Resolution*, copyright © 1984 William J. Kreidler, published by Scott, Foresman and Company.

Responding to Aggressive Behavior

1. John just took something of yours. What could you do? _____

   _____

   What might be the short-term effect of that? _____

   What might be the long-range effect of that? _____

2. Angela just pushed you hard in the hall. What could you do? _____

   _____

   What might be the short-term effect? _____

   What might be the long-range effect? _____

3. Darryl just asked to copy your homework. What could you do? _____

   _____

   What might be the short-term effect? _____

   What might be the long-range effect? _____

4. Gino is telling lies about you. What could you do? _____

   _____

   What might be the short-term effect? _____

   What might be the long-range effect? _____

5. Francine is calling you names. What could you do? _____

   _____

   What might be the short-term effect? _____

   What might be the long-range effect? _____

From *Creative Conflict Resolution*, copyright © 1984 William J. Kreidler, published by Scott, Foresman and Company.

Peace Team Cards

Set 1: School and Community

1. Grown-ups say that kids are causing all kinds of problems by hanging around downtown. Supposedly, kids steal and generally bother people. How would you attempt to solve this problem?
    If you can't come up with a suggestion, all kids will be banned from the downtown area.

2. Two groups of kids play football every recess, and every recess a fight breaks out over one thing or another. How would you attempt to make peace in this situation?
    If you can't come up with any suggestions, recess will be banned.

3. There are a group of people in your town called coopers. They are poor, uneducated, and subjected to prejudice and discrimination. They have been protesting their ill-treatment, and this has increased the number of problems they have with the larger community. How would you attempt to make peace in this situation?
    If you can't come up with a suggestion, there will be riots.

4. Kids in one house in your neighborhood have a rock band. Whenever they practice, they get complaints from the neighbors. As a result, they rarely get to practice. How would you attempt to solve this problem?
    If you can't come up with any suggestions, the band will have to break up.

5. Taxes are high in your community. Some people want to cut them in half, regardless of the consequences. Others say it is important to have good schools, plenty of police and firefighters, nice parks with swimming pools, and so on. How would you attempt to solve this problem?
    If you can't come up with a suggestion, there will be economic chaos.

From *Creative Conflict Resolution*, copyright © 1984 William J. Kreidler, published by Scott, Foresman and Company.

Peace Team Cards (continued)

Set 2: Interplanetary

1. You live on the planet Zimock. Your country needs water from a neighboring country that will sell it only at exorbitant prices. Some people in your country want to seize the water-processing plants by force. How would you attempt to solve this problem?
    If you can't come up with a suggestion, there will be war.

2. The planet Hemont has imprisoned some of your citizens who were tourists there, accusing them of being spies. How would you attempt to solve this problem?
    If you can't come up with a suggestion, they will be executed.

3. The planet of L'Okum has offered your planet mining rights which you badly need because you have few minerals. However, L'Okum people keep slaves. Some people on your planet don't want anything to do with L'Okum because of this. Others say you must have the minerals. How would you attempt to solve this problem?
    If you can't come up with a suggestion, your economy will collapse.

4. Two planets in your solar system have been fighting for years. Now they have the potential to destroy each other and are threatening to do so. How would you attempt to make peace in this situation?
    If you can't come up with a suggestion, they will destroy each other. Your solar system will be thrown out of whack, and your planet will experience great catastrophes.

5. Your planet is sending food to a starving planet. Because of government corruption there, only one-fourth of the people receive any food. Some people on your planet say that this is wrong and you should stop all food shipments. Others say that at least some food is getting through. How would you attempt to solve this problem?
    If you can't come up with a suggestion, more people will starve, and more food will be wasted.

From *Creative Conflict Resolution*, copyright © 1984 William J. Kreidler, published by Scott, Foresman and Company.

Three Musketeers Sheet

All for one and one for all!

Here are three things we all like:

1. _____
2. _____
3. _____

Here are three things we all dislike:

1. _____
2. _____
3. _____

This is how we are all different:

Name _____
How different _____
_____

Name _____
How different _____
_____

Name _____
How different _____
_____

Name _____
How different _____
_____

From *Creative Conflict Resolution*, copyright © 1984 William J. Kreidler, published by Scott, Foresman and Company.

Name _____

Comparisons Worksheet

1. **If you could do one thing, would you rather**

   ____ walk in the woods?

   ____ walk on the beach?

   ____ ride your bike?

2. **Would you rather play**

   ____ alone?

   ____ with a lot of friends?

   ____ with a few friends?

3. **Would you rather**

   ____ read a book?

   ____ listen to records?

   ____ build a model?

4. **Would you rather**

   ____ play a game with others?

   ____ cook something?

   ____ build with wood?

5. **Would you rather be**

   ____ rich?

   ____ famous?

   ____ happy?

6. **What's more important to you,**

   ____ friendship?

   ____ self-respect?

   ____ security?

7. **What's important in a friend,**

   ____ cheerfulness?

   ____ honesty?

   ____ imagination?

8. **What would be hardest for you, to**

   ____ admit you broke a window?

   ____ admit you told a lie?

   ____ say you were sorry?

9. **Would you rather be**

   ____ kind?

   ____ smart?

   ____ trustworthy?

10. **Would you rather be known as**

    ____ courageous?

    ____ creative?

    ____ adventurous?

Who has three of the same preferences?

_____

Which ones are they? _____

_____

_____

From *Creative Conflict Resolution*, copyright © 1984 William J. Kreidler,
published by Scott, Foresman and Company.

Inheritances Survey

Survey three people in the class (in addition to yourself) about having these inherited characteristics. Record the answers.

Characteristic	You	Person 1	Person 2	Person 3
tongue rolling	_____	_____	_____	_____
attached earlobes	_____	_____	_____	_____
hitchhiker's thumb	_____	_____	_____	_____
dimples	_____	_____	_____	_____
widow's peak	_____	_____	_____	_____

Place the fingerprints of your right hand here:

Fingerprint person 1 here:

Fingerprint person 2 here:

Fingerprint person 3 here:

From *Creative Conflict Resolution*, copyright © 1984 William J. Kreidler, published by Scott, Foresman and Company.

Name-calling

Have you ever called someone a name?

_____ yes   _____ no

If you answered no, think about it and try again:

_____ yes   _____ no

Why did you call someone a name? _____

_____

How did it make you feel? _____

_____

What else could you have done? _____

_____

Have you ever been called a name? _____

_____

Why were you called it? _____

_____

How did it make you feel? _____

_____

What did you do? _____

_____

From _Creative Conflict Resolution_, copyright © 1984 William J. Kreidler, published by Scott, Foresman and Company.

Prejudices and Dislikes

Do the following statements reflect prejudices or dislikes?

		prejudice	dislike
1.	Cigarette smoke smells bad.	_____	_____
2.	Cigarette smokers are rude people.	_____	_____
3.	Babies are too noisy.	_____	_____
4.	All babies smell wonderful.	_____	_____
5.	I don't like it when babies cry.	_____	_____
6.	Some teachers are unfair.	_____	_____
7.	Teachers pick on me whenever they get a chance.	_____	_____
8.	School is no fun.	_____	_____
9.	I don't like math.	_____	_____
10.	Spelling is the worst subject.	_____	_____

From *Creative Conflict Resolution*, copyright © 1984 William J. Kreidler, published by Scott, Foresman and Company.

Bibliography of Resources

Conflict Resolution _____

Adams, James L. *Conceptual Blockbusting.* New York: W.W. Norton, 1979.

Alschuler, Alfred. *School Discipline, A Socially Literate Solution.* New York: McGraw-Hill, 1980.

Carpenter, Susan. *A Repertoire of Peacemaking Skills.* Consortium on Peace Research, Education and Development, 1977.

Curle, Adam. *Making Peace.* London: Tavistock, 1971.

Filley, Alan C. *Interpersonal Conflict Resolution.* Glenview, Ill.: Scott, Foresman, 1975.

Fisher, Roger, and William Ury. *Getting to Yes: Negotiating Agreements Without Giving In.* Boston: Houghton Mifflin, 1981.

Fisher, Roger. *International Conflict for Beginners.* New York: Harper & Row, 1969.

Furness, Pauline. *Role-Play in the Elementary School.* New York: Hart, 1976.

Glasser, William. *Schools Without Failure.* New York: Harper & Row, 1969.

Gordon, Thomas. *Teacher Effectiveness Training.* New York: David McKay, 1974.

Gordon, W.J.J., and Tony Poze. *Teaching is Listening.* Cambridge, Mass.: Syntectics Education Systems, 1972.

Hoffman, James. *Critical Incidents.* Birmingham, Mich.: Instructional Fair, 1972.

Judson, Stephanie, et al. *A Manual on Nonviolence and Children.* Philadelphia: Friends of Peace Committee, 1977.

Koberg, Don, and Jim Bagnall. *The Universal Traveler.* Los Altos, Calif.: Wm. Kaufman, 1976.

Palomare, Uvaldo, and Ben Logan. *A Curriculum on Conflict Management.* Human Development Training Institute, 1975.

Prutzman, Priscilla, et al. *The Friendly Classroom for a Small Planet.* Avery, 1978.

Stanford, Barbara, ed. *Peacemaking.* New York: Bantam, 1976.

Cooperation

Aronson, Elliot, et al. *The Jigsaw Classroom.* Beverly Hills, Calif.: Sage, 1978.

DeKoven, Bernard. *The Well-Played Game.* Garden City, N.J.: Doubleday, 1978.

Fluegelman, Andrew, ed. *The New Games Book.* Garden City, N.J.: Doubleday, 1976.

——. *More New Games.* Garden City, N.J.: Doubleday, 1981.

Johnson, David W., and Roger T. Johnson. *Learning Together and Alone: Cooperation, Competition and Individualization.* Englewood Cliffs, N.J.: Prentice-Hall, 1975.

Orlick, Terry. *The Cooperative Sports and Game Book.* New York: Pantheon, 1978.

Sackson, Sid. *Beyond Competition.* New York: Pantheon, 1977.

Stanford, Gene. *Developing Effective Classroom Groups.* New York: Hart, 1977.

Wilt, Joy, and Bill Watson. *Relationship Builders.* Waco, Tex.: Word, 1978.

Communication Skills/ Expressing Emotions

Baily, Ronald, et al. *Violence and Aggression.* New York: Time-Life, 1976.

Bandura, Albert. *Aggression: A Social Learning Analysis.* Englewood Cliffs, N.J.: Prentice-Hall, 1973.

Canfield, Jack, and Harold Wells. *100 Ways to Enhance Self-Concept in the Classroom.* Englewood Cliffs, N.J.: Prentice-Hall, 1976.

Chase, Larry. *The Other Side of the Report Card.* Santa Monica, Calif.: Goodyear, 1975.

Fagen, Stanley A., et al. *Teaching Children Self-Control.* Columbus, Ohio: Chas. E. Merrill, 1975.

Hurt, Thomas, et al. *Communication in the Classroom.* Reading, Mass.: Addison Wesley, 1978.

Montagu, Ashley. *Man and Aggression.* London: Oxford University Press, 1973.

Schere, Klaus R., et al. *Human Aggression and Conflict.* Englewood Cliffs, N.J.: Prentice-Hall, 1975.

Shuter, Robert. *Understanding Misunderstandings: Exploring Interpersonal Communication.* New York: Harper & Row, 1979.

Stanford, Gene, and Barbara Stanford. *Learning Discussion Skills through Games.* New York: Citation Press, 1969.

Stone, Karen F., and Harold Q. Dillehurt. *Self-Science: The Subject Is Me.* Glenview, Ill.: Scott, Foresman, 1978.

Tolerance and Differences

Abruscato, Joe, and Jack Hassard. *The Earth People Activity Book.* Glenview, Ill.: Scott, Foresman, 1978.

Allport, Gordon. *The Nature of Prejudice.* Reading, Mass.: Addison-Wesley, 1979.

Banks, James A. *Teaching Strategies for Ethnic Studies.* Boston: Allyn and Bacon, 1975.

Barnes, Ellen, et al. *What's the Difference? Teaching Positive Attitudes Toward People with Disabilities.* Syracuse, N.Y.: Human Policy Press, 1978.

Chase, Josephine, and Linda Parth. *Multicultural Spoken Here.* Glenview, Ill.: Scott, Foresman, 1976.

Cole, Anne, et al. *Children Are Children Are Children.* Boston: Little, Brown, 1978.

Fiarotta, Phyllis, and Noel Fiarotta. *The You and Me Heritage Tree: Ethnic Crafts for Children.* New York: Workman, 1976.

Hawley, Robert C. *Value Exploration Through Role-Playing.* New York: Hart, 1975.

Johnson, Laurie Olsen. *Nonsexist Curricular Materials for Elementary Schools.* Old Westbury, N.Y.: Feminist Press, 1974.

Rainbow Activities: 50 Multicultural/Human Relations Experiences. South El Monte, Calif.: Creative Teaching Press, 1977.

Shiman, David A. *The Prejudice Book.* New York: Anti-Defamation League of B'nai B'rith, 1979.

Simon, Sidney B., et al. *Values Clarification.* New York: Hart, 1972.

Activity Index

Index

*Names of conflict resolution
techniques are capitalized.*

YORK COLLEGE OF PENNSYLVANIA 17403

0 2003 0051677 6

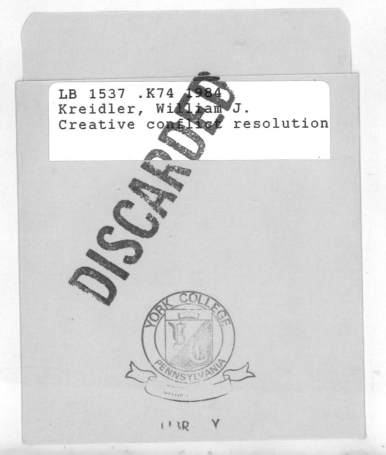

LB 1537 .K74 1984
Kreidler, William J.
Creative conflict resolution

DISCARDED

YORK COLLEGE
PENNSYLVANIA